2019

OUTGROWING

STORIES FROM THE LGBTQ+ COMMUNITY

A PUBLICATION BY COLLEGE AND UNIVERSITY STUDENTS

The mission of Writing Wrongs is to generate awareness and promote understanding of various social issues by providing an immersion experience for student multimedia journalists. They produce an entire print book and media about the specified topic in one weekend.

Published by
New Dawn Enterprises, LLC
newdawnenterprises.net

pennsylvania
COUNCIL ON THE ARTS

Contact
P.O. Box 3
Virginville, PA 19564
dawn@seekreporttruth.com
seekreporttruth.com

Social
 @seekreporttruth
@seek_report_truth
@seekreporttruth

TABLE OF CONTENTS

DISCOVERING A PURPOSE

By Carly O'Neill

As head of Reading's LGBT Center, Michelle Dech is taking strides to provide a safe space for those who are questioning, closeted, or open about their identity.

Michelle Dech had been working as a regional manager at Kitchen Collection, LLC, where she was responsible for overseeing 400 employees in 35 stores along the East Coast. A few years ago the company decided it needed to cut travel expenses. It informed her she would be spending more time working from home so she took her new-found time to explore the city of Reading after 16 years of living in it.

On the second day of staring at her home's four walls, she discovered an ad in the newspaper announcing the LGBT Center of Greater Reading was looking for volunteers.

"Holy cow, I didn't even know Reading had an LGBT center!" thought Dech, who is a member of this community. The next day she went down to the center to volunteer her time. Little did she know, this opportunity was about to change her life.

A year later, Dech found herself actively involved and on the board for the LGBT Center. When their executive director unexpectedly stepped down, she was asked to step in as full-time director. Even though she had no idea how to run a nonprofit organization, she attempted it anyway.

"I knew that it was something that I was supposed to do," she said. "I was supposed to be involved in this … It was kind of like a purpose."

It only took 28 years for Dech to come to the realization that working in retail wasn't her career path.

Then her boss at Kitchen Collection informed her that the company was conducting massive layoffs. But instead of receiving a pink slip, Dech was offered a promotion to oversee an additional 52 stores, expanding the geographic reach of her East Coast territory all the way to Nebraska. If she took the job, she wouldn't be able to continue as director at the center, as her new responsibilities would require her to constantly travel.

"I had really felt like I had found my purpose in what I was doing, and passion, and then somebody just took it right out from under me," she said.

After about two weeks of rethinking her life-long career and consulting with her wife, Dech came to the conclusion that she didn't have a choice. She requested to be a part of the company layoffs so she could continue following her calling at the Center.

"I really felt like I didn't have a choice. This was where I was supposed to be. I didn't have the answers of how it was going to work, how I was going to get paid, how we were going to keep our house … but I knew that I couldn't walk away from it. It felt that strong to me," said Dech.

In February 2019, Dech finally closed that chapter of her life and started a new one at the LGBT Center of Greater Reading as their new executive director. Six months later, she knew she had made the right choice when she was approached by a woman with her child at Reading's Pride Fest.

The mother had come over to her face painting and balloon-making tent with her almost 5-year-old son. As soon as her son was lost in activities, the mother broke down in front of Dech with only two words: "Help me."

In a span of 45 minutes, the mother informed Dech that her son was actually born a female. Around the age of 3, her son had gravitated towards boys clothes and toys, and by the age of 4, told his mom every day, "Mommy, I'm a boy."

His mother was extremely accepting and supportive of her son, but turned to Dech and the Center, since she was now at a loss of how to continue helping him. With no experience or background, she asked if the Center offered any programs for her son to get involved in.

> **❝ I don't know how this looks yet, what we're going to do, but I promise you we're going to do something. ❞**

Dech came to the hard realization that, other than therapy, not only did the Center not offer any inclusive program this mother was searching for, but no local organization did. Regardless, Dech was determined to help. "I don't know how this is going to look yet, what we're going to do, but I promise you we're going to do something," she told the mother.

One year later, Students Parents Allies Resource Community (SPARC) was created as a program for 7 – 13-year-olds and their parents or friends to socialize and connect with others in similar situations. During frequent meetings, the kids go into one room and laugh or bond through arts and crafts, while the parents meet in Dech's office to share questions or concerns.

Even though SPARC is still relatively new, the response has been overwhelmingly successful, with between 12 – 15 families participating. "It's exciting to know the program can evolve into whatever is needed to best serve the needs of the community," Dech explained. "Every day I'm very cognizant of the folks that we can help and assist."

Michelle Dech holds the hate mail she received as a result of her attempt to raise the LGBTQ+ community flag at Reading, Pa. city hall in July 2019. Dech was informed 15 minutes before the flag was to be raised that Mayor Wally Scott had now refused their request, after agreeing a month prior to allow the flag to be raised.

MORE INFORMATION

The LGBT Center of Greater Reading is a non-profit organization.

It's been in establishment for three years.

It offers a variety of services:
- nine support groups, two of them specializing in youth
- professional development
- training for various businesses, school districts and police departments
- reference and referrals for lawyers, doctors, etc.
- advocacy work

They currently partner with more than 30 different agencies and organizations throughout Berks County.

They host annual events throughout the year:
- game nights
- senior lunches
- community events like Pride Fest

The LGBT center is currently working closely with the city of Reading to raise awareness of LGBTQ+ rights and diminish sexual and gender discrimination.

Learn more at:
https://www.lgbtcenterofreading.com

WHAT DO YOU SEE ?

By Mia Boccher

JO'E SIMONS

Jo'e L. Simons had just retired from their prior job as an educational administrator when their parents and godfather passed away.

It was then, at the age of 63, that Simons realized they were not female. It wasn't their makeup or their hair that was wrong when they looked in the mirror. It was their gender. In this period, Simons realized he was trying to be someone he was not for the sake of his family.

"I really need to get out of this box," he said. "So I did." It wasn't easy. Simons had always been such a "good girl" growing up, doing everything expected of them. Growing up in California with a Naval officer father and country club mother, Simons was following the path set up for them to be a girl, a wife, and a mother. Simons followed that path for a long time, and now they honor those past and future lives with their current name.

"My business name is Jorie, and if you take out the r and the i, add an apostrophe. (It makes Jo'e.) It honors my female name and my newborn male name," he said.

Today, Jo'e L. Simons is a 65-year-old trans-masculine person living in Reading, Pa. Depending on the day of the week, Simons' pronouns are he/him or they/them. Simons looked in the mirror quite a lot when they were a female-presenting person. Their wife would jokingly call them vain, but Simons just wanted to look because something felt wrong. Was their hair okay? Was their makeup okay?

Now that they've become the person they've always wanted to be, they admit that they still look in the mirror but not as frequently, and only to check if they have any whiskers and to make sure their hair isn't out of place.

Sitting in lawn chairs outside the LGBT Center of Greater Reading with Simons, we talked about his experience within the LGBT community as cars sped by.

Now that Simons is retired, he works as a community educator with Safe Berks, which is the local crisis center for domestic violence and sexual assault, and as a training director at the LGBT Center.

Simons has done training in a multitude of areas and communities, and he likes to start training the same way each time.

"I come out as trans in every training I do because I feel it is important to people to put a face, a person, to a concept," he said.

The LGBTQ community, or affectionately called the alphabet soup by Simons, is such a large acronym due to the immense number of words describing orientations that people feel connected to. He recognizes that all these words are extremely nuanced and hold special meaning to people.

Working with transgender youth and older people in support groups has strengthened his belief on this. While helping others express who they are and supporting them in that process, there is almost a common language for transgender and non-binary folk due to the social, medical, and legal processes they need to overcome to be who they are and the person they want to present to others.

"Gender, to me, is expressing myself who I want to be along or off the spectrum of male or female," Simons said. "It's definitely not a binary and I think it differs for different people in different stages of life."

  There needs to be more education on pronouns ...

Sexuality is a more individual experience, but Simons said that like transgender and non-binary folks, it can be a unifying factor for groups.

It's obvious when the "L's," or lesbians, all hang out in one group and the "G's," or gays, hang out in one group. They don't mean to isolate, they just have a shared connection based on their orientation that makes them feel comfortable or safe, he said.

Simons compares the experience of the LGBTQ community to a pendulum. It has to swing from one side to another before it can balance out. The '60s were a part of LGBTQ awareness that focused on gay and lesbian individuals who eventually reached acceptance. Currently, transgender and non-binary people are facing a hard time gaining acceptance, but Simons believes it can be achieved.

"It's just about people," he said.

For non-LGBTQ allies, he asks for anyone to ask him any questions instead of making an LGBTQ person uncomfortable. For LGBTQ individuals like himself, he wants to reassure them that it is okay to be making waves.

There has been no negative feedback since Simons has transitioned. He politely asked people to unfollow him on Facebook if that was an issue, but he feels supported and safe.

The only issue is that there needs to be more education on pronouns, due to it not being so familiar to some individuals, specifically hospital staff.

"I just went through some medical stuff and in my chart, they do have my preferred name and that I am transgender. The first thing they do is refer to me as "she." Do I choose to say something or do I choose not to?"

If at a local hospital, he opts for explaining. At a hospital that is not local or regular, Simons chooses not to talk about it.

"It's really important for me to express who I am," said the 65-year-old interviewee. Yet, at times, it is easier not to get into specifics with people who do not understand. "The hope is that the future looks to be open to anywhere LGBTQ people want to go." Simons has taken that hope of the future by sharing their story as a way to encourage others to do the same.

"Maybe it will help someone else. I felt like I have hidden my whole life who I truly was and I want to be more visible in this way."

Friends Ezra Isaac-Kenobi Feliciano + Jo'e Simons have fun outside
the LGBT Center of Greater Reading between interviews.

EZRA ISAAC-KENOBI FELICIANO

" And when I found the LGBT community, they uplifted me and I uplifted them. There's no other way to explain how I feel but empowered. "

AN IDENTITY IN FLUX, A COMMUNITY IN SUPPORT

By Gillian Russo

The days of "half-coming out" are over for Ezra Isaac-Kenobi Feliciano. They may still be realizing their identity, but they're ready to own it.

"I still identify as non-binary," said Feliciano. "It's a personal thing for me. I want to fully be able to start transitioning — at least, I want to be able to start T [testosterone] — before I sit here and say I'm transgendered ... I do believe I am a man, but you know, society isn't always nice when people say that. So 'they/them' is just easier."

There was no one turning point at which Feliciano came to terms with their identity. Rather, their ability to come out resulted from many interactions through which they built a community network of support.

The support fortunately began at home. When Feliciano first "tested the waters" by coming out to their family as bisexual, their mother was supportive. However, she remained cautious about broadcasting the news due to the risk of outside prejudice.

"Even though I knew at the time I was a pretty strong lesbian, I came out as bisexual," remembered Feliciano. "I had a girlfriend at the time, and my mom was like, 'Hmm, we're going to have to keep that hush-hush. You can't tell anyone that kind of stuff.'

"I understand where she was coming from back then. Like, I was really young, you know, people in society are just assholes, and she was just trying to protect me at that time ... It was hard, though, because I felt like I couldn't talk to her."

Soon, Feliciano brought their concerns to their mom, who quickly suggested talking to her "like you talk to your friends." As Feliciano shared more about their identity, they were surprised at how knowledgeable she already was on LGBT topics.

"In the beginning, it was rocky," Feliciano admitted. "But as I got older and was able to explain how I felt more to my mom, she was able to pick up. Like when I came out to my mom — halfway again — I was like,

'Mom, I'm non-binary, and that means — And she interjects. She goes, 'It means you don't consider yourself a woman or a male.' And I was just like, 'Oh, wow! You know that?'

"Now I can talk to her. I remember, two weeks ago I was putting up a new curtain for her ... and we were talking about top surgery like it was the most normal thing ever. And it felt great."

Feliciano grew up in a Catholic household, but religious beliefs were never a source of bigotry in their home. However, the attitudes of other Catholic people made them re-evalute their own relationship with religion as early as elementary school. They recalled one instance in which a girl in gym class told them they would go to hell for not believing in God.

"Outside of my house, it was always shoved down my throat that God hates gays," said Feliciano. "There was a time in my life where I struggled with who I was and was like, 'This isn't who I am because God put me in this world, and God hates gays.' And then there's part of my life where I was just like, 'Well, if God hates me then I hate him.'"

Although they do not currently identify with the Catholic religion they were raised with, Feliciano was able to rekindle their relationship with God.

"Fast forward ... throughout high school, I realized that I am who I am. And if God is real and he put me in this world, he put me in this world knowing damn well what he was putting in this earth. So therefore, I can love God, God loves me for who I am and everything's chillin'!"

Feliciano also named their friend Scout as a major source of mutual support. The two attended the same high school but never talked until they both attended Spectrum, an educational program for LGBT people. There, they discovered that Scout, too, was transgender, and the two grew close over their shared experiences.

EZRA ISAAC-KENOBI FELICIANO + JO'E SIMONS

"The things he felt ... were the same things for me, like it was just echoing," Feliciano said of getting to know Scout.

"I was just like, 'Wow, I can actually live my truth now.' So honestly, it's been really thanks to Scout."

Aside from Scout, Feliciano connected with even more transgender people at an LGBT summit in Detroit earlier this year.

"I went to the sections of the transgendered stuff and I was just like, 'Wow, what the fuck, this whole room is full, and it's not just me,'" Feliciano recalled. "Everyone who told their story, I could pinpoint a moment in my life where I was just like, 'That happened to me, too. I felt that exact same way. Yes, yes, yes, this is all making sense to me now.'"

The summit also made Feliciano intimately aware of the hatred transgender youth face.

"Ever since then, I've been wanting to bring more attention to the transgender community. But I've also seen a lot of hatred ... I've, like, physically experienced it more.

"I feel like the moment I went to the summit, got that information, and I came back home was the moment when my eyes actually opened up to the world. I felt

like I was wearing these rose-colored glasses; I felt like they finally came off."

These interactions sparked Feliciano's interest in advocating for others in their situation. Their first concrete opportunity to do so was a job educating high schoolers as part of a Latino organization. It forced the Puerto Rican-born Feliciano to examine the intersection of their gender identity with the Latino community.

"They were supposed to be uplifting the Latino community, LGBT community ... however, when I was working there, they were very homophobic," Feliciano said. "I wanted to do a meeting [about] how to properly bind your chest without causing harm. And I told my director that during a staff meeting, and she looked me dead in my eye and told me, 'Better have that on a Saturday when none of the other ladies are here.'" They recalled that people would use homophobic slurs to describe the meeting. When Feliciano tried to confront other staff members about it, nothing would happen.

Feliciano has since quit that job, but they miss the young people they had the opportunity to lead. Their desire to bring attention to others' struggles has now led them to study social work at Reading Area Community College, where they are on the path to turning their interest in advocacy into a permanent profession.

"My mentor, Bethany, very kindly told me that social work is like activism, but with a steady paycheck," Feliciano quipped. "So that is what I'm doing."

It's important to Feliciano that, just as the discovery of a community strengthened them, they do all they can to be a welcoming, active resource for others.

"When I was struggling with my identity, I felt really weak and hopeless and alone," said Feliciano. "And when I found the LGBT community, they uplifted me and I uplifted them. There's no other way to explain how I feel but empowered."

Feliciano specifically spoke to support for transgender health. "My whole ability to be able to transition and start testosterone is because my insurance is paying for it." If their insurance recalls that coverage, Feliciano said, "I can't transition, and I'm not going to be okay as a person.

"I have friends that are struggling and going to multiple different therapists ... and if they take all that away from us ... suicide rates are going to rise."

According to a 2019 study by the Trevor Project, 54% of transgender and non-binary respondents have seriously considered suicide, and 71% of all the LGBT respondents reported feeling sad or hopeless for at least two weeks in the past year. Through continued advocacy, Feliciano hopes to connect with others and do whatever they can to decrease these statistics — one step to fully and confidently coming out at a time.

EZRA ISAAC-KENOBI FELICIANO

TRENT BAYNE

TOM, BOY'

By Steve Hernandez

As a child, Trent Bayne felt he never fit in with women, and he didn't fit in with boys. "They didn't want to look at me that way. I wanted to hang with the guys, I wanted to smoke cigars, I wanted to look at cars … They just thought I was a tomboy, and now I'm like, 'Hey, I'm Tom. I'm a boy.'" Then Trent grew up, and for the ten years he was a police officer he was treated just like one of the guys.

Trent figured out that he was a man about two years ago; previously he presented as a masculine, lesbian woman. "I went to therapy, and I picked this therapist out, basically, because she had a dog." He was unaware that the therapist he chose specialized in transgender issues. One day, Trent saw the previous patient, a trans man, walk out of his therapist's office. His heart began racing as fast as his thoughts, an epiphany brewing, and he finally thought, "I think that's what I am." His therapist later told him that she knew the day he first came to her office.

Trent worried that coming out as trans would make life difficult for him, his wife, and his kids. He worried that his children would be picked on at school, and that his wife would face even more discrimination than she previously had as a lesbian woman. He didn't worry so much about himself. He resented the idea that he felt like he couldn't be himself for the sake of his family, and he took it out on them. "But I wasn't angry at them — I was just angry. Let's just let me deal with the hurt. I've had 58 years of it." Trent had finally figured himself out. He came out, but was still scared that his life would worsen — that he and his family would be ostracized and discriminated against, that his family wouldn't accept him, and resent him for all of it.

"But it hasn't been that way." His two young children call him daddy. His daughter told her teacher that "Momma T is a man now," after which the teacher offered her support by texting Trent: "If there is anything I can do to help, please let me know." In a new job at Metropolitan Edison, Trent's coworkers are entirely accommodating. On his first day of orientation, they made sure they got his preferred name correct. When he told his boss he was unsure of which bathroom they wanted him to use, they offered to build him his own bathroom, if he wanted — he declined, and the other male employees ensured him that they were comfortable with him in their bathroom.

Trent does a considerable amount of educating people, and he is happy to do it. He often catches people staring at him with inquiring, curious eyes. They seem terrified to offend with a question that sounds too ignorant, so he feels free to say, "Go ahead and ask! I know you want to. If you ask, then that fear of 'Oh, I'm going to say the wrong thing' is gone." And when people misgender him, he understands, saying, "Sometimes I misgender myself!" The thought of growing facial hair, developing a deeper voice, and growing broader shoulders excites him. Not only because it will make him more comfortable in his own skin, but also since it will then be easier for other people to think of him — to gender him on the fly — as a man.

The two people Trent thought for sure would turn their back on him, his brother and sister, are the most supportive of all his family members. However, Trent's brother still does not call him by his name. Trent says this doesn't bother him, but he wishes that he "would just say it" — to admit that it's hard to think of his sister as a man. Caught up in the idea of his sister is the idea of Trent as a girl, and Trent appreciates that it's not as easy as turning a switch on and off. But he makes clear, "I'm still me … my soul is still me." Trent remains the same person — the only thing that has changed is his understanding of himself.

It brings Trent joy to help young people discover how they identify. He has the following advice for everyone who is unsure of themselves:

"If you're feeling something and you don't know what it is, talk to somebody about it. And if that person doesn't want to listen, find someone who will … Whatever it is that you are, you have to talk about it, because it'll kill you, it'll destroy you, and it'll destroy things that could have been. I had a lot of that anger: it could have been different. What would I have been doing? Who could I have been? What would I be now?"

TASHA SANTIAGO

RECONNECTING

By Kimberlee Bongard

Tasha Santiago, 26, assists in facilitating youth support groups for ages 7 – 21 at the LGBT Center of Reading. Santiago brings an intimate level of understanding to the specific age group because she came out as a lesbian after her teen years ended.

"I felt like I never had that guidance that I hope the youth get from us," she said, explaining why she applied to work as an intern at the Center beginning in January 2019.

Living in the heart of downtown Reading, Santiago also attends Bloomsburg University online, pursuing technical design. Her responsibilities at the Center align with her ultimate goal of pioneering her own nonprofit that would serve the LGBT community.

When facilitating support groups alongside Board Director Sarah Morin, she assists in lesson planning and fosters conversations about mental health, sexual health, and maintaining healthy relationships.

For teens struggling with their sexuality or identity, she advises them to stay true to themselves and come out at their own pace.

"Be careful, and the most important thing for anybody is to be true to themselves and know themselves," said Santiago. "You don't need to share yourself with the world. The world doesn't need to know your story. They might not even deserve your story. It's really up to you whether you want to share it."

When Santiago came out at 20 years old, she was suppressed with feelings of isolation, stuck in a bad relationship, and lacked a community of close friends to confide in. The lack of personal connection and compassion led her to attempt suicide.

"There were people I've known for years that suddenly changed because of [coming out], and I had been the same person. And then there's some people who didn't mind and didn't even think it was really news," Santiago recalled.

Reflecting on the severe moments of isolation she experienced, Santiago reframed it as a rebirth that allowed her and her parents, who were not initially accepting, to reconnect and gain mutual understanding for each other.

Santiago explained that much of her parents' reluctance to accept homosexuality is rooted in Spanish culture and the stigma surrounding gay Latina women.

"It's mainly, 'We don't talk about it. We acknowledge that you're that — okay, whatever, but do not bring it up. Do not talk about it. We don't speak about it. If you have a partner, that's your roommate. That's your friend for life. Never acknowledge them as your significant other.' That kind of erasure is damaging," Santiago said.

Despite the looming stigma, her parents have embraced her sexuality and underwent their own personal growth in developing compassion for the LGBT community, most recently wearing shirts that say "Free Mom and Dad Hugs" to a gay pride festival this year.

"They'd rather have a gay child than a dead one," Santiago said. "Once they realized that, they tried really hard to get to know more about the community and were open to discussions and took apart their feelings," Santiago said.

As a white-passing Latinx woman, Santiago classifies her own struggles as low-scale compared to people with darker skin tones and is concerned about the severe challenges LGBT people of color face.

"LGBT people of color and trans people are being targeted, and I feel that their safety is important. There's a genocide against these people and not enough is being done. Not enough focus is on it. Week after week, there's a new person up on the obituary who was brutally and wrongfully murdered," Santiago said.

Her concerns are even more prominent considering suicide rates are also higher among trans people of color, according to the "2015 U.S. Transgender Survey." She encourages people to use their platforms to bring awareness to issues related to safety and inclusion.

"If you don't even really have much of a platform, you most likely have more of a platform than they do, so if you use what little platform you have, I feel that's helping in the crusade to equality."

Despite the challenges that members of the LGBT community face, Santiago admires younger generations' passion for advocacy and activism. She looks forward to seeing more change ignited in the near future as a result of widespread LGBT representation in everyday life.

"There's more representation in the movies and in TV shows, but it might not be enough. We need representation in politics," she said. "We need representation in the system, in our schools, in our local government because we know they're everywhere; it's just they're not being represented or shown or visible."

A LOVER + A FIGHTER

By Mia Boccher and Gillian Russo

For Aries Franklin-Ortiz, being pansexual is a part of what makes her Aries. The 34-year-old facilities manager came out as gay at 16 years old, which has led to labeling herself as a lesbian, bisexual, and ultimately pansexual. As a half Puerto Rican and half black woman, Franklin-Ortiz's immediate family was very accepting. Both sides of her family, she said, embrace the idea that "you're going to grow into being who you want to be, no matter what." They advocated for her and supported her as she came out. Before long, Franklin-Ortiz began to accept herself, too.

"I always feel like our timelines are meant to be a certain way," said Franklin-Ortiz. "So had I not been pan or gay or lesbian or whatever — even if I was straight, I'd still be where I'm supposed to be."

Although she is confident in her identity now, she originally questioned herself. Eight years of Catholic school brought conflict for Franklin-Ortiz, as people "beat it into" her that she would be "going straight to hell" if she identified as gay. She was angry at 13 years old and fought a lot before coming out — that was, until she discovered the "loopholes" in the Bible. After it condemns homosexuality, it also forbids a man from cutting his hair and eating shellfish.

"And you shouldn't eat pork," she also said of the Bible's rules. "I'm half Puerto Rican, so we live off pork. So I was going to hell either way ... I might as well love who I want to."

Being Puerto Rican and LGBT comes with its own set of challenges. When she visits Puerto Rico, she must hide her identity in certain towns, particularly Ponce, in which people would be hostile or even violent towards her. In addition, relatives outside her immediate family — who are also traditional Catholic Puerto Ricans — know about her pansexuality but believe it goes against the family's Catholic values. (Franklin-Ortiz's main counterargument is that those family members had just eaten pork).

Franklin-Ortiz wishes that her community in Reading, Pa., showed their support in larger ways beyond "a little sticker in the window," such as flying a rainbow flag or holding a pride event outside the town's small park. She is grateful, though, that the environment is one where she need not fear being insulted walking down the street or discriminated against in a store.

Franklin-Ortiz bluntly said she'd be either crazy or dead if she had a less supportive family, friend group, city and community. Her mother did cry when she came out, but solely because it would be harder for her daughter to navigate the world. Being an LGBT person in addition to already being female and a person of color (POC) stacked the odds against her, and her mother knew that.

ARIES FRANKLIN-ORTIZ

Franklin-Ortiz has now found herself understanding her mother's concern. Jeydon, her 16-year-old son, recently came out as transgender.

He struggled in their former home in Womelsdorf, being angry and listening to dark music. The mom admitted to being worried about her son for a while, but said he is happy now. She would remind him to "stay strong" because she can't always be there to protect him as much as she tries to keep him safe. Her advice, rooted in the fact that her son has already been confronted by boys in school, highlights the reality of intimidation transgender people face.

Franklin-Ortiz said she would tell Jeydon: "I do think you'll get stronger … but you've got to stay strong through it no matter what because men will mess with you. And it's sad to say, you're going to have to defend yourself no matter what."

Now home-schooling him, she believes they are all in a good space. Franklin-Ortiz devotes a lot of her time to her three step-children, whom she co-parents. She also collects vinyls, listens to music, attends poetry sessions and art shows with her son, volunteer-coaches basketball, goes on camping trips, and writes.

Formerly a freelance writer, Franklin-Ortiz is currently writing a fictional novel based on her real-life experience coming out. She hopes to expand people's understanding of sexuality through her own journey.

To her, gender and sexuality "is nothing. It's just a word; it's just a definition … People are going to love who they want to love … And as it is, they're going to identify as they want to identify."

Within the LGBT community, it can be hard being pansexual. According to Franklin-Ortiz, some of her friends who like people of the same sex are not 100% accepting of bisexual or pansexual people.

This stigma is not irregular in the community, with bisexual and pansexual folks told to "choose a side" or that they are "not gay enough" to be LGBT but "not straight enough" to be heterosexual.

If a friend doesn't support her or disagrees with her, she takes them out of her life.

"It's a part of who I am. People have to accept it," Franklin-Ortiz said. "I mean, I don't care if people don't like it. That's not my problem; it's theirs. But you're going to respect me regardless. I'm going to do what I want to do, and you can't stop me."

She is hopeful, though, that the future will hold more universal acceptance for LGBT people. She sees the new, younger generations' growth as an opportunity for new ideas to take root.

"Everything is changing, from cell phones to taking trips to space," acknowledged Franklin-Ortiz. "We're going to be accepting of everything … I think that right now, people are putting up a fight because they're [the] older generation … And as the generations switch, and as everything changes, it's just going to be easier for people to accept.

"It's a fight now, but everything was a fight at one point."

Above all else, the one thing Franklin-Ortiz is fighting for is to freely live her life as a woman who loves a woman.

"You can put whatever label you want on me," she said. "I'm still just Aries."

Aries Franklin-Ortiz (center) is interviewed by Staff Writers Mia Boccher (left) and Gillian Russo (right) outside the Hampton Inn, Wyomissing.

"It's a fight now, but everything was a fight at one point."

ADAM NOUR VAROQUA

HIS QUEER REVOLUTION

By Kristen Marcinek

Adam Nour Varoqua,

a 22-year-old graduate from Seton Hall University and a native of Haledon, N.J., first heard about a link on his school's website to the conversion therapy organization, Courage International, through his friends. His first reaction was, "What? No way!?" Varoqua then vowed to have the link removed from the school's website.

Conversion therapy, as defined by the Human Rights Campaign, "is a range of dangerous and discredited practices that falsely claim to change a person's sexual orientation or gender identity or expression." According to the American Psychological Association, it is unlikely that conversion therapy "will be able to reduce same-sex attractions or increase other-sex attractions." These factors are why Varoqua knew that he had to do something about this situation.

He commenced his efforts to get it removed by emailing members of the Diversity and Inclusion Committee on campus, tenured faculty members, and members of the administration. He said he had "no sense of support from administrators," but did from students and faculty. It took him many email attempts and different campaign tactics, including social media and pamphlets, to drive his point home. He even wrote a personal letter to the Monsignor he met with in which he described his opinions on the matter and that it was imperative for this link to be removed. He marched to the Monsignor's office, donning his rainbow cape, and hand delivered it to him. While a struggle, Varoqua eventually won his battle against Seton Hall's administration.

Despite his victory, Varoqua felt disrespected by administration. His initial meeting with them had not gone well. All he wanted was an apology. While never having received one, he forgives the Monsignor he spoke to, stating, "I do forgive him for my sake ... I do have this weird faith, weird hope, this weird inclination that people can change."

Varoqua's true out-and-proud story begins in his freshman year of high school. When first coming out to his parents, he declared himself as bisexual. He recognizes this as a fallacy now, but at the time he believed it was more palatable to his conservative parents. Varoqua sputtered out his coming out speech while riding in the back of a car. "My mom said, quote, unquote, exact wording: 'I'll fucking kill you,'" spoke Adam.

This most certainly "struck a nerve" with him. The experience was a traumatic one and made him stay in the closet until junior year.

"I had my first boyfriend there. Sweet guy; very, very sweet guy; really helped me a lot," expressed Varoqua. On their first date, his mom and her friends drove by their car. "I'm like, please, please act straight, please act straight, and he proceeds to not act straight," he recalled.

Later on in the night, Varoqua and his mom proceeded to have an argument regarding his sexuality. This was his second coming out. Varoqua's third coming out to his parents happened a year later during his senior year. He left a note on his bed for his parents to discover. Adam describes his mother's reaction as "completely not accepting." He continued: "You need to think of Sodom and Gomorrah ... I just need to be more religious."

Eventually he claimed that "there was sort of this weird cycle where I would come out to my mom, or parents in general, they would get mad about it, they would forget about it ... and so on and so forth."

> **"He marched to the Monsignor's office, donning his rainbow cape, and hand delivered it to him."**

Arriving at Seton Hall in 2015 was another step in Varoqua's journey as a gay man. Seton Hall was a transformative experience for him. Varoqua hoped that Seton Hall would bring new beginnings, even if it wasn't his first choice. It wasn't long before his hopes were shattered. "It was worse than I thought," he said.

Both Varoqua's troubles and victories began when he went on a tour of Seton Hall campus. He noted that there wasn't any LGBT+ presence on campus. "There wasn't even any flyers or posters," he stated.

The tour guide informed him of a club, Allies, which he soon learned was not what it seemed. Varoqua learned this through visiting the university's involvement fair, where Allies was not anywhere in sight.

Allies, the only LGBT+ club at Seton Hall, had a tumultuous history. In the 1990s, having a gay-straight alliance (GSA) at Seton Hall was struck down by the administration on religious grounds. Students tried for a GSA again in the 2000s, where they were accepted as a student organization, but not officially. There were many strict regulations put upon the organization as well as a lack of official funding and standing. The administration made the GSA change their name from Truth — as it was too close to God's word — to Allies.

Varoqua was not very involved in Allies his first two school years. The first meeting he attended his junior year "was just the President, the Vice President, myself, and that was it." He quickly became involved on the organization's executive board and wanted to bring the club to official university standing with the Student Government Association.

Spring of his senior year he was promoted to the role of President. "I was pushing for us to do more, more presentations, more advertising. … We started to build a membership back up," explained Varoqua. The last thing he pushed for was to get Allies to official university recognition. During his quest to gain recognition, the College's Ministry requested that Varoqua and Allies meet with the administration. "They said, 'Hey, listen, we want you to get recognized,'" Adam explained, "'but there's going to be pushback from the priests in the community.'"

Administration gave Varoqua and Allies an offer: they could be officially recognized, but they had to include stipulations within their constitution that their activities would align with the teachings of the Catholic Church regarding sexuality. Varoqua "begrudgingly" accepted the offer and quickly had that clause voted out of the constitution.

Once administration caught word of the vote, they added another clause. This time, they added that it could not be amended. When he left the club, they had voted out the "do not amend" clause and have now become an officially recognized club.

Through all Varoqua's conquests, he remembers the true reasons why he fights: the LGBT+ community. "I'm proud of our community. I'll always be an advocate for the queer community. We are deserving of equal rights. No matter if anyone is in the closet or fully out, you're beautiful; you're valid," he said. "You deserve acceptance and to be loved, celebrated. That's what we fight for every day, is to be accepted, to be celebrated for who we are, and not to be ashamed of who we love. At the end of the day, being queer is a revolutionary act."

By Kristen Marcinek and Gillian Russo

WANDER

Janny Simmon has made many stops
in their life's journey. They have had jobs in industries
from fashion to landscaping to, currently, restaurant
service. They have traveled all across the United
States and even gone beyond its borders as far as
Germany. Ultimately, their travels have now landed
them right back in Pennsylvania near where they
grew up. The memories attached to this area aren't
the fondest, but Simmon can now look back on them
from a slightly more positive place.

Simmon grew up in a conservative environment —
both those in their household and at their school
were forthcoming about their dislike for LGBT
people. When Simmon began to realize they
were gay at age 11, they remained closed off,
kept their identity secret, and ended up feeling
lonely and afraid. Their mom and brother would
speak about "faggots this and faggots that"
with enough disdain to make Simmon consider

Staff Writers Gillian Russo (left to right) and Kristen Marcinek talk with Janny Simmon at the Hampton Inn, Wyomissing.

running away from home. However, school was even worse — the other students wrote comments on the walls, threw things at Simmon's house, and made comments that were far from meaningless insults.

"I got threatened by several kids — they're going to put me in the woods and shoot the shotgun," said Simmon. Luckily, the students never acted on these threats, but Simmon had to quit school for the sake of their mental health.

Bombarded by negative attitudes towards their homosexuality, Simmon turned to the church for a while. At the expense of embracing their identity, they tried to "find God and get free."

"Who wants to go to hell?" Simmon said of the reason behind their decision. Yet, they did not find the peace they were seeking among the church members: "Even they find out eventually. I've tried to go to certain people in church that I thought I could trust, talk to them … But as soon as they found out you're gay, they couldn't talk to you, just like that." Simmon has since turned to Native American spirituality, intrigued by its basis in nature. This interest was sparked by their stay in Texas — the place where, out of their many travels, they did find a vibrant, positive community.

Simmon remembers their time in Texas as one of the moments when they felt most proud of their identity. They recalled that in the Dallas–Fort Worth area, where they lived and worked for two years, nobody mistreated them for their sexuality. In fact, they and the group of people they met there found places to celebrate themselves, including Simmon's favorite: the Rainbow Lounge.

The Rainbow Lounge's history evokes that of the famed Stonewall Inn (an especially timely comparison in light of Stonewall's 50th anniversary this past June). The Lounge was

a thriving gay bar complete with "drag shows and DJs and karaoke" in a section of Fort Worth known for gay bars. On the 40th anniversary of the Stonewall riots, the venue experienced a police raid that sparked a protest. The Rainbow Lounge would eventually end up burning down in a faulty air-conditioning accident, and Simmon misses it and the scene there. They eventually had to leave Texas to be with their family back up north.

Simmon's mother had been an ambivalent figure in their life. Simmon describes their mother as having had negative feelings towards the LGBT+ community. During the 90s and 2000s, their mother "came around" to the LGBT+ community through the media. During this time she developed cancer and has recently passed.

Simmon's mother was a source of support to them later in her life. When she left their life, Simmon and their mother had been on good terms. Upon hearing the news of her passing, Simmon moved back to Pennsylvania.

Nowadays, Simmon's support network is small but steady. They mentioned their boyfriend of eight years as an important figure, as well as their coworkers at the pub, who have met their boyfriend and accept Simmon's sexuality.

The LGBT Center of Greater Reading offers a free clothes closet for community members to "shop" for clothing relating to their gender identity and expression.

Simmon's experience has also consistently intersected with the internet, for better and for worse. It has been — and can be, for other LGBT people — an outlet through which Simmon has found a community in times when those in their life did not provide it. For example, they met their boyfriend as well as the person who would eventually invite them to Texas on Gays.com, an online community for gay men.

The internet was also the platform for another one of their proudest moments: publicly coming out.

"I went bravely on Facebook, because I was on the church website, and I just put out a blank statement that said ... 'I'm gay,'" said Simmon.

They acknowledged, though, that the internet's community capacity has a dark side. It also amplifies oppressive voices and false information, especially in the midst of a turbulent political climate and "divisive" issues regarding LGBT rights.

"It's a really divisive issue and people are wanting, I think, to perpetuate that divide," said Simmon. "If people only look at just one side, they're going to get all the wrong information. So I guess what we all need is to make sure we're trying harder to get the right information out."

When asked about what advice they would give a younger LGBT person, Simmon expressed the importance for younger people to communicate with those who understand them. "There are groups out there that have notice now. I would encourage anybody to find one of these groups and go talk to them," Simmon continued. "It doesn't matter if you're in fear or your family is against it. Before you do anything else, talk to them. Talk to somebody who's been there. Do anything; get connected with people who care about you and what's best for you." And if someplace lacks acceptance, there's always nature to wander through and new horizons to explore.

NAVIGATING YOUR TRUE SELF

By Kimberlee Bongard

When Sarah Morin, 41, joined the Board of Directors at the LGBT Center of Greater Reading in April 2019, there weren't any LGBT support groups organized specifically for youth. In a matter of months, Morin began leading a weekly discussion for transgender youth and launched a youth group at the Center.

"I've always been supportive of the LGBT community. I didn't quite realize I was part of it for a long time," Morin said. She became a transgender member of the LGBT community after undergoing a male to female transition last year.

After visiting the Center twice this past year, Morin found herself volunteering and helping out wherever she could and discovered when she's working with kids or helping people, it didn't even feel like work. "It's amazing to find a place where you feel completely comfortable, and you know there's going to be no judgement. A big part of my acceptance and my transitioning was learning I could do things to help others and become involved with other people."

Morin is a seventh grade social studies teacher in the Muhlenberg district and found that her passion lies in advocating for youth. When Morin applied for the Board of Directors position at the Center in April, she sought to increase the Center's inclusivity by implementing more youth programs.

"I really wanted to do things to support LGBT kids. In many ways, I think they're a lot more vulnerable than LGBT adults. Kids can sometimes be more accepting than adults, but at the same time, I see it in school

that there's still a lot of homophobia and transphobia," Morin said.

Morin still hears the insensitive outdated slang, "That's so gay," echoed in her classroom settings. Despite this hostility, she said most students are progressing toward awareness and amiably call fellow students by their preferred pronouns.

Undergoing her own personal transition journey motivated Morin to get more involved with individuals who are struggling to understand their own gender identity.

"Prior to transitioning, I was suicidal. I was hospitalized for a while, and while I was in the hospital, it was really scary, especially the very first day, but I learned pretty quickly that by going to groups and talking to other people that I would be helping other people," she said.

"In many ways, that really was the key to my emotional recovery and my mental recovery. By helping others, I did help myself and gave myself a sense of purpose."

Before transitioning, she remembers herself as an introvert who was content going to work and returning home to watch television. But once she started volunteering at the Center, she began looking for more ways to get involved with the community in addition to setting personal goals for herself.

"When I first made the decision to transition, I thought I was just going to transition my gender, but I didn't realize that my personality was going to change too," Morin said.

SARAH MORIN

In the current political climate, Morin said many transgender individuals, including herself, feel pressured to get their transitions done before the operations may be systemically revoked. However, the rushed methods of care can lead to complications as severe as death for transgender individuals.

"Once people have a civil right, it's usually not taken back away, but we're in the position now where we didn't have protections and rights and then we did, and now we're at the point of being afraid we're going to lose those protections," Morin said.

"We're in a situation now where more people feel comfortable enough to be themselves despite the fact that we're still rejected by a lot of society."

Despite being outed by a colleague, she was quickly accepted by the other women she worked with and was invited to girls' nights, forming even closer bonds with them.

Although her mother and father accepted her, Morin's kids and ex-wife had a more difficult time coming to terms with her transition. Through therapy, she realized suppressing her true self was the root of the anger she wielded in her home and personal life.

"The longer I went of denying myself who I was, the more depressed and anxious that I got and angrier that I got," Morin said.

"It was a risk that I was going to lose all my friends, all my family, my job, my home, everything. But when the alternative to that is death, it makes losing those things a lot less scary than dying. That was really what influenced my accepting myself."

For people who are struggling with gaining acceptance, Morin encourages them to fake their confidence until it manifests itself as genuinely real confidence. She also encourages people to immerse themselves in any kind of activity whether it's LGBT related or not, simply for the joy of being part of something larger than yourself.

For Morin, writing poetry and running a blog on Medium is her way of exploring LGBT and trans-related issues. Prior to transitioning, she recalls following people on social media and online who had successfully transitioned; she now realizes they saved her life in many ways.

"When I write, I want to use my words and my ability to write to let people know they're not alone in how they feel and [to] inspire people."

Staff Writer Gillan Russo interviews Jillian Hyde at the LGBT Center of Greater Reading.

A GIRL WHO LOVES A GIRL LIKE ME

By Gillian Russo

"The whole world stopped, and it was just her."

So thought Jillian Hyde when she first laid eyes on Danelle Bower. As in an endearingly cheesy romance novel, the feeling would turn out to be mutual: "She knew she couldn't exist in a world that did not have me in it. That's what she told me and I'll never forget that," Hyde recalled.

The two met when Hyde was 20, a student in Bower's class at Wilson College. After two semesters of "miserably" bottling her infatuation, Hyde reached out with an invitation to her 21st birthday party — and to her surprise, Bower accepted. There they shared their first kiss, and now that a teacher-student barrier no longer stood between them, they began to open up about their feelings for each other. There was still one problem: Bower, still closeted, was married to a man.

"She married her best friend from college," Hyde said. "Her family loved him. So it was really hard to win over their hearts because they were still heartbroken from that loss, which I understand ... And of course, with her coming out, they looked at it like it was my fault. They saw me as the enemy at first. And since then we've grown ... it was rough, but eventually they accepted us and they accepted me."

Hyde and Bower are now married and living in Shoemakersville, Pa., with two children: 12-year-old Brooklyn and 10-month-old Julian, and they hope to grow their family soon. As they inherited Brooklyn from Hyde's sister as a toddler, carrying Julian was the couple's first experience with pregnancy. The time was not without its challenges, especially for Hyde as the carrier. As a masculine-presenting woman, one of her greatest difficulties was finding maternity clothes she felt comfortable wearing.

"I had a lot of anxiety about it," Hyde said. "I don't feel comfortable in women's clothes. They just don't fit me ... I feel like it doesn't represent who I am."

"Every single thing in the maternity store [has a] scoop neck and thin straps and all this kind of stuff. And I'm trying on a simple tank top ... And I looked so ridiculous. I looked in the mirror and I just — I just started crying and laughing at the same time. It was one of these moments where I felt so discouraged, but also embarrassed, but also I could find the humor in it."

She extensively searched for clothes online, too, to no avail. She read about one startup company focused on maternity clothing for masculine women, only to subsequently discover it failed to launch.

"There's literally nothing for girls like me," Hyde recalled thinking.

American Eagle's stretchy pants and Under Armour's extra-long shirts came to her rescue. That was a start, but the element of human affirmation was still missing. She and Bower soon found that, too, in a parental-care "centering group" they joined. Hyde was fearful at first that she and Bower might experience discrimination or "funny" looks. The opposite occurred.

"I was so happy that I gave it a chance and I didn't let fear stop me," said Hyde. "I learned so much, and we had just a good vibe."

The one time her sexuality was the subject of a joke, it wasn't at Hyde's or Bower's expense — its mention was normalized, and the group was able to laugh together. Hyde chuckled at the memory: "You can get pregnant right after you have the baby ... So they talk about preventative measures, like what you do, what's your form of contraception. They had cards, and they laid them out and people would stand next to whatever card.

"So the coordinator was looking at the cards, and she looked at a certain one. She started cracking up, and she was looking right at me. I'm like, 'Dude, what?' She turned it over and it said 'No sex with men.' And I'm just dying. I'm like, 'There it is. That card was made for me.' And everyone just started laughing ... it was just one of those lighthearted moments."

Being in the presence of other expecting mothers, both with experience and without, was crucial in

alleviating some of Hyde's fears. But there were some that she couldn't shake. Having been raised solely by her dad, Hyde worried the absence of her mom would affect her own motherhood.

"I seem to take on ... 'the father role,'" Hyde said. "The protector of the family. And it's kind of where I shine because I'm a lot like my father ... I was worried that I wouldn't have that maternal instinct, that I was lacking since I didn't have a mom."

The presence of the "nurturing" Bower, who Hyde believes "was born to be a mom," uplifted Hyde through it all.

"It just comes naturally to her," said Hyde. "All of her students — they, you know, lean on her and confide in her and she nurtures them, and she kind of is the 'village mom' ... And being able to watch her and see how she mothers [Brooklyn], and just to see what a good, healthy connection with a motherly figure looks like — I'm really blessed to see that."

Upon Julian's birth, Hyde discovered that her own maternal instinct did come naturally, too. She also found herself grateful for her pregnancy in that it affirmed her identity as a woman to others.

"That was the other thing about being pregnant — at least people didn't shoo me out of the bathrooms," Hyde said. "But when you look like me ... I can't tell you how many times I've gone into a bathroom and had people make comments to me, yell at me, scream at me."

Now that she is no longer pregnant, her voice assures people that she is female, in bathrooms or otherwise. Hyde wishes others would understand and accept her identity without seeing a pregnant belly or hearing a feminine voice.

"A question that my whole life I've kind of gotten [is], 'Why do you dress like a boy?'" Hyde said. "My answer is, I don't dress like a boy. I dress like me and what feels comfortable and what fits my body ... And it's not that I want to be a boy. I don't feel like I'm a boy. I'm proud of being a woman."

This woman has Bower, and she has children, and from them, she has love. Amidst a world that's judged her family as much as welcomed them, that's all Hyde really needs.

WE'RE HERE, WE'RE QUEER, WE HAVE ALWAYS BEEN HERE:

Historic Events in LGBTQ + community

1920s

1924 Henry Gerber forms the Society for Human Rights, the first gay activist group in the United States, and publishes *Friendship and Freedom*, the first known American gay publication, but the group and the publication are quickly shut down.

1926 The *New York Times* is the first major publication to use the word "*homosexuality.*"

1950s

1950 The Mattachine Society is formed by activist Harry Hay as one of the first gay rights groups in the United States.

1955 The Daughters of Bilitis (DOB), considered to be the first lesbian rights organization, is formed by Del Martin and Phyllis Lyon in San Francisco, California. The group is conceived as a social alternative to lesbian bars, which were considered illegal and thus subject to raids and police harassment.

1960s

1961 Homosexuality is decriminalized in Illinois, the first state to do so.

1962 Illinois becomes the first state to remove sodomy law from its criminal code.

1963 Bayard Rustin, noted civil rights activist and gay man, is the chief organizer behind the historic March on Washington, which culminates with Dr. Martin Luther King, Jr's famous "I Have a Dream" speech.

Photo taken by Rhododendrites

1969

Police raid the Stonewall Inn in New York City in the early hours of June 28. This leads to four days of struggle between police and LGBT people. Transgender people, LGBT people of color, and youth are a major part of these "riots" that mark the birth of the modern LGBT movement.

1970

The Pink Triangle resurfaces as a gay pride symbol. The Naz[i] used it in WWII to ident[ify] gay men in concentrati[on] camps.

The first Gay Liberation Day March is held in New York City.

1970s

"LOVE IS LOVE"

2017

The Trump Administration repeals the Title IX Obama-era guidelines protecting trans students in the United States.

2016

President Obama dedicated the new Stonewall National Monument in Greenwich Village, Lower Manhattan, as first United States National Monument to honor the LGBT Rights Movement.

1977

Harvey Milk becomes the first openly gay person elected to public office in California when he wins a seat on the San Francisco Board of Supervisors.

2015

The Supreme Court rules that states are constitutionally required to issue marriage licenses to same-sex couples, legalizing marriage equality in all 50 states.

2001

Vermont legalizes civil unions between those of the same sex.

The Netherlands is the first country to legalize same-sex marriage.

1978

Gilbert Baker raises the first rainbow flag at San Francisco Pride. It had eight stripes.

2000s

Keith Haring, 1958 – 1990

1980s

1998

Tammy Baldwin became the first openly lesbian candidate ever elected to congress, winning Wisconsin's second congressional district seat over Josephine Musser.

The first bisexual pride flag is unveiled.

1982 Nearly 800 people are infected with GRID (Gay-Related Immunodeficiency Disorder). The name is changed to AIDS (Acquired Immune Deficiency Syndrome) by the year's end.

1987 ACT UP (AIDS Coalition to Unleash Power), a direct-action activist group, is founded in the LGBT Community Center in NYC to bring attention to AIDS-related issues using civil disobedience.

1996

Congress and President Bill Clinton approved the "National AIDS Memorial Grove Act," which officially set aside the de Laveaga Dell land in Golden Gate Park to be the site of the first AIDS memorial in the nation.

1990s

NO HEALTH, NO CARE

By Kristen Marcinek

In 2015, Krista and Jami Contreras were excited to take their 6-day-old child for her first pediatrician visit. When arriving at the practice, they were greeted by a different doctor who relayed to the Contreras's that their chosen doctor could no longer see their child. The doctor explained that the original doctor felt that after praying on it she could not form a "normal" patient-doctor relationship with the couple and their child.

This is one of the stories that Danelle Bower, an associate professor at Reading Area Community College, presented when she spoke to students in the Writing Wrongs program at the LGBT Center of Greater Reading about physical and mental health among the LGBT+ community. This is a story that was of note to Bower, as she has a wife and two children.

Bower is passionate about and conducted research on the issue of LGBT+ healthcare. Bower wants to raise awareness on lack of access, or as she calls it, "gaps" in the community. "Inclusivity is the first step, but then equity also has to be there," she said. To Bower, there are three big "clusters" which represent the issues with healthcare in the LGBT+ community. "One is health disparities," she said. "Areas in which the LGBT community, on certain measures, is more likely to have higher incidences of particular illnesses and conditions."

Suicide and suicidal tendencies among LGBT+ individuals are an urgent issue, Bower declared. In a 2019 survey by the Trevor Project, 39% of respondents "seriously considered attempting suicide in the past 12 months" and "more than half of transgender and nonbinary youth have considered suicide." For LGBT+ adults, the National LGBT Health Education Center in 2018 found that they "have a two-fold excess risk of suicide attempts compared to other adults. Among transgender adults, the lifetime prevalence of suicide attempts is 40%."

Another issue faced by LGBT+ people is outright discrimination, such as denial of coverage and health services. Eight percent of LGBQ individuals reported that they were refused healthcare due to actual or perceived orientation, and 29% of transgender individuals were refused care due to actual or perceived gender identity, according to a 2018 Center for American Progress study.

Bower revealed that while she never suffered outright discrimination, she did experience a microaggression after undergoing induced lactation to breastfeed her and her wife's child. The induction was needed because her wife carried the child.

Once, when her son was in a Central Pennsylvania hospital, a doctor referred to her as a "milkmaid." "I don't think he meant it to be hurtful at all. I try to think people come from a place of kindness … but it was very, very hurtful," stated Bower. This is how microaggressions make people feel; though one feels they cannot blame the other person due to that person's ignorance or lack of malintent, they are still offended.

Being referred to as a milkmaid is not the only experience Bower brought to the table. Drawing upon her own experiences as a social worker and a professor, Bower shared LGBT+ case studies with the attendees of her speech and asked them to come up with systemic-level solutions. Some of the discussion prompts included problems in "disenfranchised" grief or grief unacknowledged by society, assisted living, misgendering, suicide, and denial of care.

A common solution suggested by students for resolving some of the health challenges involved offering sensitivity training to medical staff. Bower agreed but said policy level change is needed as well.

"My opinion as a social worker is that change has to be on kind of this micro level. So one-on-one you educate practitioners and how to provide culturally competent care," she continued, "but it also has to be on this policy level. … You've got [to have] existing law that can hold them accountable."

DANELLE BOWER

LILLIAN MUNSCH

COMING ACROSS

By Steve Hernandez

"I'm 71 years old and I've lived a lie as a male for 68 of those years." Lillian Munsch is a tall, blonde woman who radiates kindness. Her handshake and smile are gentle, while her voice solitarily dominates the room. "I had, by all accounts, a normal childhood. I tried to keep busy so that my mind wouldn't rest on what was going on within me." When what was inside her couldn't stay there, she snuck into her mother's room and wore her clothes. When mom came home, Lillian would be lying in her own bed, in her boy clothes, praying that she would wake up as a woman. She kept praying all the way through college.

When Lillian graduated college, she married a woman, hoping a wife would efface these problems. "I figured, well, I'd get married and it would cure me of this." It did no such thing. Living independently with a liberal income enabled Lillian to buy her own clothes — women's clothes. Her routine continued, but now Lillian had to hide it from her wife. Her wife eventually found them and confronted Lillian about it. "I promised her I wouldn't do it again. But of course, I couldn't. I tried as hard as I could to not think about being a woman. Not to think about dressing up. Just trying to be what society wanted me to be. It just didn't work."

Lillian tried to research her condition — searching desperately for a label, so that she could determine what was wrong with her. "I figured it was something that was wrong, that I did something or something afflicted me that I could deal with and put it aside, but it just never happened."

In 2016, Lillian couldn't put it aside anymore. She swallowed a bottle of pills, hoping she would never wake up. She did, in the hospital, where psychiatrists swarmed her. According to the US Transgender Survey, 40% of transgender individuals attempt suicide at some point in their life. Lillian eventually found her own therapist whom she felt more connected to. When Lillian saw her for the first time, "It was like the dam burst." She had never spoken to anyone at length, honestly, about her desires to be a woman. Lillian was not aware that there was such a thing as "transgender," and that there were so many people who felt just as she had her whole life. The mere knowledge of the concept helped her to find people like her.

Shortly after Lillian came out to her wife, her wife tried to commit suicide. Lillian came home in time and took her to the emergency room. After her wife recovered, she filed for divorce. Lillian recommended a different solution: "I felt guilty and responsible for her attempted suicide, and for her feeling the way she did about me, so I suggested to her that we remain married, but live apart. That way, I could still provide her with medical coverage."

The day Lillian's wife filed for divorce, she moved out. That same day, Lillian began her transition. "I immediately started living as a woman." And she immediately felt liberated, finally like herself.

Lillian's wife takes every effort to avoid seeing her. They have a son together, who is married with two children. When he hosts a birthday party, or when holiday celebrations come around, Lillian's wife first asks their son if Lillian is coming. If the answer is "Yes," she does not attend. The only communication between Lillian and her wife takes place over email, where she refuses to address Lillian by her first name — but refers to her only by her last, "Munsch." Lillian has tried to get through to her wife, to get her to at least listen, to no avail. "I still have hope that maybe one day she'll understand, or at least try to understand, and maybe we can get on at least a talking basis. I'm holding out hope, but I really don't think it's ever going to happen."

Lillian's son has said that he accepts her new identity, but that he doesn't understand it. Lillian is sympathetic to the idea that "it's difficult to just sort of spring this on someone." But her son and his wife treat her like a woman, without coddling her. They treat her like a normal person.

Lillian's friends at first said that they were accepting of her — that they would support her. They used to go out to a bar every week, get a drink, and chat. One week, they stopped calling Lillian to tell her they were going to the bar. "It just sort of went away." Now Lillian gets invited to their annual fall and Christmas parties, but their relationship is fractured — these friends whom she has known for 35 years.

But Lillian is making new friends. She attends TransCentralPA meetings and helps organize their yearly conferences — where trans people from all over the world (as far as South Africa) come together to bond. Lillian even considers one girl she met at TransCentralPA her best friend: "We're always there for each other." With all the people Lillian has met through TransCentralPA, she has built a symbiotic support system. "I know I could count on them if I needed something."

Lillian has two pieces of advice for people struggling with their identity today: (1) Take advantage of the resources available to you. (2) Find someone to talk to in order to help you adjust and love yourself. "You have to like and love yourself before you can go out and come across to other people."

"You have to like and love yourself before you can go out and come across to other people."

The manuscript for Tyler McMasters' article "Dysphoria Distillation, a Letter of Change" for the HerStory Campaign.

WHAT IS GENDER IDENTITY?

By Carly O'Neill

Gender Identity is not only something members of the LGBTQ+ community grapple with, but it's also something society is quick to put expectations on. If you dress and appear as a man, does that mean its okay for someone to label you as one in a public setting? Does the phrase "What's up, man?" now carry a sort of assumption behind it?

Tyler McMaster provided more insight into this topic as an individual who identifies as a trans-feminine, someone who is born male but relates more with the female side of the gender spectrum. McMaster uses the pronouns "she" and "they" and graduated from Kutztown University in December of 2018. She is a former Writing Wrongs staff writer from the 2018 domestic violence and sexual assault year.

There are many common misconceptions of the LGBTQ+ community that stem from our culture's assumptions of how men and women should act from a young age.

McMaster found that the biggest hurdle for many people is empathising with what it feels like to be born one gender but identify with another. Ultimately, McMaster wants to gradually transition to make herself appear more feminine, but at the same time go against what everyone expects based on her appearances.

"I could opt in and be what this one expectation of me is, but I also know that humans are not like that, and to expect humans to act one way or the other is ridiculous," said McMaster.

For most, the main reluctance of being open about their pronouns or gender identity in public is the fear of eliciting a violent or objectifying response. McMaster expressed her concern about this, since she can never be too sure if she's going to be in a comfortable or dangerous environment.

McMaster recognized that it's hard to train one's brain to comprehend experiences that an individual has never had. As long as people show an effort to correctly identify a person of the LGBTQ community by their preferred pronouns or orientation, they're communicating their respect for that person without even realizing it. Long story short, gender is complicated.

"I think gender is important ... I think the ways that our culture and our overall structures view it is very liminal ... and not good, because most people think that sex and gender are the same thing, but it can be this very important aspect for some people," McMaster elaborated.

Three years after graduating from community college in 2013, McMaster found herself back in college as a commuter, working towards a bachelor's in English with a professional writing minor. At Kutztown University of Pennsylvania (KU), she worked closely with the Feminist Majority Leadership Alliance on campus, and this organization became her family.

"Once I graduated there was this brief feeling of losing a sense of community. That sense of safety that you had is suddenly not quite as there anymore," McMaster commented.

At KU, McMaster decided to mix it up. Instead of taking routine classes like she had in the past, she enrolled in an E-news Around the World class. When she got there she was only one of three guys at the time in the class and immediately her doubt kicked in. She decided to sit in the back of the room to give the rest of the women in the class a voice.

A couple classes in, the professor went up to the board and wrote two words: "Sex" and "Gender." Sex is biologically understandable, she said. Then she went over to "gender" and described this term as "a pile of bullshit."

This was the turning point for McMaster. She finally realized she could put her gender under a microscope to examine all the pieces that made this word whole. McMaster wasn't just a "tomboy" or a "goth" kid; she was a whole new identity that she was excited to explore.

McMaster's first introduction into the trans community was when Laura Jane Grace, the lead singer of the band Against Me, came out as a transsexual in 2012. "That was huge, because I was just, like, what? This is a thing that people do? Wow! I was like, that's super awesome," McMaster elaborated.

Their release of True Trans in 2013 quickly became one of McMaster's favorite albums. Even though she didn't fully understand how she fit into that trans community, she loved Laura's story and the power behind their lyrics.

McMaster described this new reckoning as a hallway full of doors that were mostly shut until recently. Once she started having discussions of gender in class and pondering what this new outlook of identity meant to her, they finally flew open.

HerCampus was another transformational outlet for McMaster, who decided to join on a recommendation. She attended the first meeting and was already expected to have an article written up by the following day. Instead of scrambling to come up with content, McMaster finally forced herself to put down on paper what she had been struggling to articulate for the past couple of years.

She entitled it Dysphoria Distillation, a Letter of Change, and her words spoke wonders. McMaster mustered up the strength to let the world into her subconscious, and refused to let her fears hold her back.

> ## "There was no turning back at that point."

"There was no turning back at that point," said McMaster.

Most recently, McMaster joined Lehigh Valley Girls Rock, an organization that has youth and adult summer camps for female trans and non-binary individuals. The camp offers two adult camps; one takes place over two months, the other over a weekend.

This past July, McMaster volunteered at Girls Rock Camp for youth campers. This program takes place over a week, but the ties she made continue to last. "They kind of became my new space and new family to kind of work within when I wasn't in school anymore. At first it's kind of like, how is this going to go? I know how I appear to the world; how are these people going to receive me? They've been so incredible ... they just treat me as I expect to be treated," McMaster continued.

Going forward, McMaster believes raising awareness about LGBTQ issues, beyond Stonewall, is an important step in changing perceptions and overcoming discrimination.

"The biggest thing I would like to see is more education available to anybody. Just have the resources there and have them teach about these sorts of things in classrooms, so that people start to understand," explained McMaster. "These kids aren't coming in completely blind."

LOVE, MOM AND DAD

By Mia Boccher

Jennifer Hanf and John Loomis' twin daughters Tricia and Belinda both came out as members of the LGBT community during Belinda's college graduation weekend in 1997. Tricia came out on Saturday and Belinda came out on Sunday.

Hanf and Loomis' daughters are now in their mid-40s with children of their own.

During the interview in Reading, Pa., Tricia sent Hanf a text, recalling her father's reaction 22 years ago to her news of being gay.

"With great care and a deep level of seriousness, Papa said, 'Tricia, I always have and always will love you unconditionally.' I don't know how many times I replayed those words in my head. It's countless, but I have fallen back on them as the most serious and loving words someone has spoken to me," Tricia wrote in a text Hanf read out loud before having to turn the phone over to her husband after becoming too emotional to read more.

Tricia is married to a woman with two children in Northampton, Mass. Loomis and Hanf explained that Tricia and her wife each had one of the children biologically through the same sperm donor. The two children are half-sisters and because of this have a joint last name that flips depending on which mother borne who. One daughter borne of Tricia, Rio, has the name Loomis-Santos and the other daughter has the last name Santos-Loomis.

Gender and sexuality are concepts that are difficult, Hanf and Loomis said. The two admit that they grew up in the '50s when certain gender roles were enforced. Loomis had a childhood in Detroit of riding bicycles and throwing rocks at friends, while Hanf was taught to iron napkins.

Loomis is glad that his grandson won't be raised like him. His grandson is more creative and encouraged to draw and play with blocks unlike Loomis' upbringing.

The concept of role models and growing up with a diverse group of people is incredibly important to the grandparents, specifically because their grandchildren can become whomever they want to be. This wasn't an option for Hanf and Loomis in the past.

"The people who couldn't fit in, in many cases became clinically depressed," Hanf said. "I mean, how do you live when there's no role model for you?"

It was all kind of expected for Loomis and Hanf to fulfill female and male roles with their mothers essentially raising them to perpetuate these roles. That is why they are willing to adapt to the asking of pronouns for transgender and nonbinary youth, but still feel it is new and foreign to them.

"The concept of asking someone their pronouns, I didn't hear about that until six months ago," said Loomis.

"It's all new to our generation," Hanf said.

If socialized when younger, Hanf believes that she may have been a different person. The 66-year-old believes if for not being raised in a certain way, she may have used they/them pronouns and would have identified as "somewhat asexual."

Loomis is a retired astronomy professor and Hanf is a retired graphic designer. Hanf continues doing activism work through a course she developed that focuses on anti-racism at the Reading Quakers building. It is a public course held once a month,

John Loomis and Jennifer Hanf speak with Staff Writer Mia Boccher at the Hampton Inn, Wyomissing.

and a second course is starting up soon that will focus on training a diverse group of people.

"When there's still racism going on around liberals, it seems to me that we ought to solve that problem right where we are," Hanf said.

Dialogue is important to Hanf because of the diverse and racialized community that is in Reading, Pa. and within their own "blended" family. Hanf shared that she knows a lot of people her age who are horrified at having a family with LGBT and people of color members. It is a major reason why Hanf and Loomis wanted to talk about their experience as LGBT parents and as grandparents with children of color.

Their daughter Belinda is bisexual, married a Haitian man, and has one son in Brooklyn, NY.

Within the LGBT community, race is a divisive topic and something that the grandparents worry about, with so many police shootings of unarmed black men and the rise in hate crimes.

Ezra, their 5-year-old grandson, mentioned one time how he was glad he wasn't black due to the violence and issues people of color face.

Even though Loomis and Hanf's children and grandchildren are safe and being educated, the grandparents say they can't help but worry.

As LGBT parents, Hanf and Loomis' mentality grew from expecting their kids to become a certain mold

and grew up not talking about things that were different to being more open and flexible. A few decades ago, the future of LGBT children was more "opaque" due to lack of rights and respect. Loomis said he felt a sense of disappointment when his daughters came out because he was afraid they had condemned themselves to a difficult life. Hanf worried their lives would become harder in regards to marriage and children. However, they now feel that the neighborhood, schools, and community where their daughters live are safe.

In the same text to her step-mother, Tricia shared her advice to LGBT youth as an elder. "I don't know if this is important for queer youth, but because it is likely that many of them are not hearing this message from their parent, maybe what's behind this message is the hope and the belief that everyone deserves unconditional love, and if they are not hearing it from their parent, they can trust someone important will give them that message."

To parents with LGBT kids, Loomis and Hanf say embrace your children, that there is nothing to fear, but a lot to look forward to. To LGBT kids, Loomis and Hanf repeat their daughter's advice to find a community and make a family with people who will accept you and friends who will support you.

Loomis and Hanf came to talk about their daughter Tricia, but left saying that every LGBT child is "deserving of love and respect how they are, exactly as they are."

CONNECTING THE RAINBOW

By Steve Hernandez

Christopher Paolini, 33, has played guitar for over twenty years. In school, he was active in choir, plays, and musicals. At heart, he is a thespian: he wants, fundamentally, to "make people feel something." He has performed his own pieces through Reading Theater Project's 5 Minute Fringe Festivals. He also has been performing professionally in drag for 15 years. Paolini began appearing in January at public libraries in Wyomissing through Drag Queen Story Hour (DQSH), where he reads stories and sings songs to children in his drag persona, Amie Vanité.

Paolini, by fourth grade, was told regularly by his classmates that he was gay. In eighth grade, his school held a contest to see who could give the best oral presentation. He gave a speech about how he was definitely not gay, and won. He came out the next year. Since he attended Catholic school, the teachers began mistreating him, until one particularly irritable nun pulled Paolini into her office. She accused him of leaving apple cores in light fixtures — he is allergic to raw apples. Chris had had enough, told the nun "Fuck you," and spent the rest of the school day turning in his schoolbooks to his teachers. He finished his diploma at a public school.

His father was disappointed in him for being gay. He had tried to force Paolini to play baseball and basketball, while Paolini most enjoyed going over to his neighbors' houses and playing dress-up with the girls. "I just loved wearing flowing things that I can twirl around in."

Paolini's father sent him against his will to a camp for youth with mental illnesses. The resident psychiatrist wondered, "What do they want me to do, give you a straight pill? I don't have one." He sent Chris home.

Paolini's mother, he says, was "upset, but I didn't really understand why until I was older … her upsetness was coming from a place of her being afraid for me, for my safety, and for my health." Otherwise, she has always been supportive.

After high school, Paolini spent two years at Kutztown University of Pennsylvania studying acting. He expressed his exhaustion over how many boys felt the need to confide in him in college: "I'm always that person who has to help them figure out who they are … by making out with them."

Paolini was disgusted with how theater professors would continue to teach those with no innate acting ability. He felt, just by teaching these bad actors, it is akin to telling them that they can act, when they will never be able to. Some people, he believes, just don't have it, and "you can't just pull it out of your butt." He felt that he wasn't learning anything, surrounded by too few talented actors and too many overly obliging professors. He dropped out, but not before founding Kutztown's first drag show. They invited him back several years following to perform.

After college, Paolini became more involved in the local drag scene. In July of 2018, Paolini founded the local chapter of DQSH. In January, he had his first gig at a library in Wyomissing as Miss Amie Vanité. Since then, he has had several other appearances where the room was full to capacity.

Drag Queen Story Hour seeks to give children fabulous, queer role models. When Paolini heard about DQSH, he wanted desperately to do it, since for him, "drag always just felt normal." When he was young, he adored the splendor and joy of "The Wizard of Oz" and "The Nutcracker." He wanted to look like Dorothy and Clara, so he would dress up as them when his grandmother watched him.

The children who visit him see him as normal, despite being different. The protestors who come to DQSH events do not. Paolini has said that the protestors are not violent, but have told him that he is living a "wrong" life, and that he is confusing children about gender.

Christopher Paolini treats Writing Wrongs staff to the stories and music of Drag Queen Story Hour. For a little while, everyone was five again.

Christopher Paolini sings "Rainbow Connection" from the 1979 hit film, "The Muppet Movie."

Paolini believes that what is more confusing for the children is the adults who denounce people like Paolini for being a boy in a dress — while the children seem to understand that he is simply "a boy in a dress" and nothing more. Children will approach him in his neighborhood, when he is out of drag, and refer to him as Miss Amie.

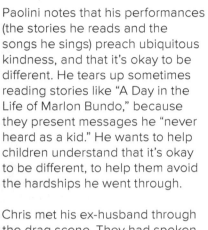

Paolini notes that his performances (the stories he reads and the songs he sings) preach ubiquitous kindness, and that it's okay to be different. He tears up sometimes reading stories like "A Day in the Life of Marlon Bundo," because they present messages he "never heard as a kid." He wants to help children understand that it's okay to be different, to help them avoid the hardships he went through.

Chris met his ex-husband through the drag scene. They had spoken multiple times at other shows, and he made Paolini "feel safe," although Paolini knew that he was dating someone else. One day at a drag show, Paolini, his ex-husband, and his ex-husband's then-boyfriend spoke privately. The boyfriend said "I want to see other people, so I'm leaving you. He (pointing to Paolini) is in love with you." This is how Paolini and his ex-husband began their relationship — hardly willingly.

Paolini was abused by his husband "in every possible sense of the word." He broke his hand, choked him, and split his lip several times over and on different occasions. He decided that the two of them should date together — forcing Paolini to bring a third man into their bed. Paolini didn't want to — he wanted to only have sex with his husband. But he also wanted to make his husband happy. The husband coerced Paolini to have sex with their new boyfriend frequently, afterword scolding Paolini for cheating. Then they would get a new boyfriend, then another, and then another. Eventually, a boyfriend moved in with them. Paolini's husband began dating him instead and kicked Paolini out of the house.

After being expelled from his home and his marriage, Paolini received calls and texts from strange phone numbers asking if he was feeling okay. These phone numbers belonged to his ex-husband's ex-boyfriends. They told him stories about their experiences with Paolini's husband, experiences that were identical to his own. He would enter into a relationship, convince his partner to bring a third into their bed, and eventually leave the first for the third.

Paolini notes that he didn't think anything was wrong for the ten years they were together, since his parents' relationship was so dysfunctional. He goes through copious amounts of therapy for abuse and trauma counseling and is easily triggered by small reminders of his ex-husband. This makes intimacy, even at the most basic level, hard for him.

Paolini moved in with his grandparents after his husband kicked him out. To compound his struggle, they both subsequently died within a year of each other. "It's hard to navigate all of these emotions that I never expected I would have to feel in such a limited window in my life," he said.

It's difficult for Paolini to be in their house, sorting their things, doling them out to the appropriate relatives. His grandparents were both singers, and they gave him the most valuable tools he has. "My grandfather instilled in me [the] technique to be a good entertainer," a tool he uses while acting, in and out of drag. "My grandmother instilled kindness in me," a tool he uses to teach children during DQSH. Paolini's grandmother was a devout Catholic, but never treated him with disdain like the nun he swore at. His grandmother was "an open book with open arms for everybody." She loved him unconditionally, telling him, "God doesn't make junk."

Miss Amie Vanité is helping normalize people who have historically existed either in secret or at the margins of society. Not just for children, but for the adults who bring their children, and the adults who are intrigued at the concept of DQSH. To normalize Miss Amie is to normalize difference, to instill in children a habit of treating queer people first as people, and second as queer. Behind Miss Amie is not just Christopher Paolini, but the lessons taught to him by the two most important people to him: his grandma and grandpa. "It all comes from them. They are living through me now. Yeah, it's Miss Amie, but it's really not anymore. It's the two of them."

Chris is being true to himself and performing in a way that would make his grandparents proud, teaching children that it is okay to be themselves. "When you're true to yourself, that resonates with other people, and you find support where you didn't know you had it before."

HOW WE ALL WIN

By Mia Boccher

"Conservation is about preventing waste, and waste can be land, air, water, human capital, and thought," said Laure Larkin, a scientist and LGBTQ volunteer. As human beings, we have a responsibility to be aware of the waste we emit into the world, including the waste of ignorance.

Larkin works for Ethicon, a subsidiary of Johnson and Johnson, as an associate director for the Stability Program. An example of her job is making sure that sutures are strong enough to be used in surgery. She also volunteers at the The LGBT Center of Greater Reading and has been interested in conservation "before it was cool." At the Center, she focuses on suicide, bullying, and isolation among youth and the elderly.

"One is our future, and the other is that we owe a debt to them for the past," she said.

The older generation understands the positive and negative power of labels, as does the younger generation but in a different way, said the 56-year-old woman.

"The youth are trying to rise above the labels and be known simply as the human species," said Larkin. And as the human species, we are responsible for conservation.

Althogh she recognizes that labels are valuable for funding purposes, identifying research, trying to do a data-based approach, and focusing on groups that are struggling with discrimination, she hopes that one day they will be unnecessary.

"We don't need them for male, we don't need them for female, we don't need them for black, white," she said. "We will all identify as being within the single tribe of humanity rather than the lesbian versus the gay versus the trans."

Until that happens, Larkin believes that labels are important in identifying her authentic self. Without labels, she would be driven back into the closet, which is the last thing she wants.

On a beautiful late summer day, Laurie Larkin speaks with Staff Writer Mia Boccher outside the LGBT Center of Greater Reading, housed in the Evangelical Lutheran Church of the Nativity.

Laurie Larkin speaks passionately with Mia Boccher, staff writer.

"We're just normal people who want to be treated like normal people, respected, dignified, and contributing members of society who care about what happens on this planet," she said. She believes views can be changed by making connections, which is a big reason why Larkin felt motivated to tell her story. A wife, mother, and community member who loves history, science, her pets, traveling, and advocating for sentient life, Larkin is more than just a lesbian.

At the time of the Writing Wrongs workshop, Stonewall had just celebrated its 50th anniversary while the Supreme Court was set to review LGBTQ discrimination on the basis of religion. Against this backdrop of celebrations and challenges, Larkin still believes the future is bright for the LGBTQ community.

But more needs to be done to recognize the mostly forgotten transgender, bisexual, black, and brown family members in the LGBTQ+ community. One idea is to add black and brown stripes to the rainbow flag and flying the transgender flag as a way to highlight their inclusion. Everyone needs validation, she said. Unification is very important to the LGBT Center and to Larkin. This is seen with youth groups and older groups coming together for game nights and having fun together.

"With a lot of LGBTQ young people facing depression and anxiety, it's easy to feel isolated," she said.

"I feel like when you're young and in high school, you're so emotional and that the negative things that happen feel like they're permanent," Larkin said. "And that feeling of permanency causes kids to take their own lives. And every life lost is an opportunity lost. It goes back to conservation."

According to the Trevor Project, LGBT youth are three times more likely to contemplate suicide than their heterosexual counterparts.

Larkin talked about growing up in La Crosse, Wisc. and, like most LGBTQ members, abused substances as an adolescent. She was angry at being unable to conform to the Midwest heteronormative lifestyle she grew up with.

This experience allows her to relate to the young people she works with in Reading, so she repeatedly tells them they matter and that they will change the world.

The scientist in Larkin is trying to figure out a way where everyone, animals and humans, can win. The world, she said, needs all of us.

COMING OUT TO MYSELF

By Carly O'Neill

HALEY MARTIN

In the process of examining her sexuality, Hayley Martin discovered she might be bisexual. This realization made her down a bottle of pills. She knew she needed help and turned to her father. She was 14 when she was first driven to the hospital.

This led Martin to an inpatient program, in which she found herself three different times while she was in high school. During one of those five-day programs, she revealed to the support group that she might be bisexual.

"I struggled to figure out my sexual identity and just my own identity in general," she said.

During this dark period, Martin was grateful to have the support of her family along the way, especially her father. Throughout her journey of discovery and perseverance, Martin's dad never let her forget how important she was to him.

"He would look at me and tell me that I'm one of the strongest people he knows while I was sitting in a hospital bed," said Martin.

Martin elaborated on the internal struggle she and many others fight with when going through a state of depression. She would constantly think to herself, "I'm alone; I'm alone." Eventually she started to believe it and isolated herself from her loved ones.

During her recovery, Martin couldn't help but always feel like suicide was her backup plan. After her third attempt at it, she realized she was meant to be here; she couldn't leave her family like that. Between sophomore and junior year was her last visit to the hospital.

Haley Martin (right) speaks with Staff Writer Carley O'Neill outside the Hampton Inn, Wyomissing.

"I'm not just living for myself," said Martin.

Her biggest fear about coming out as bi was being judged and not accepted, especially by her mother, who embraced her with open arms. She describes the first time she had told someone she was bi in one of her hospital visits as, "It felt right; it felt good."

Martin always felt like she dressed more masculine, but when she acknowledged her bisexuality, she knew she didn't want to lose sight of her femininity. This led her to find that her pronouns are she and her.

"Coming out to myself was my biggest struggle and I fought myself on that for a long time, but when I finally embraced it, it was this moment of clarity," she said.

Now as a proud 20-year-old, this experience has allowed Martin to avoid the fear that others face in the LGBT community and normalize her sexuality. Being more open has allowed Martin to overcome her doubts in discussing her identity with others.

"I'm very grounded in being a woman; I'm very proud of that. I also feel like it's a good thing that we're breaking those stereotypes; people can just be people," she said. "If you dress one way it doesn't make you this or that; you're just a person."

Martin found a family in this new community that accepted her before she even accepted herself.

Most recently, Martin graduated from The Culinary Institute of America and is now working as a line cook. She eventually plans to go back to school to study nutrition.

Going forward, Martin would like to see more representation of the LGBT community in government and positions of power.

"Hopefully we can get more diversity in our government," said Martin, "because as America we are very diverse people."

BE VOCAL AND VISIBLE

By Kimberlee Bongard

"**It wasn't** anything to do with my work. It wasn't anything to do with me. He was just uncomfortable having a gay man in his office," said Mark Stanziola, recounting the struggles that came with balancing a life as a lawyer and a gay man during the 1990s.

Stanziola's personal story of workplace discrimination is unsettling, especially to the Writing Wrongs staff, a volunteer group composed of college students who reached adulthood during a decade that celebrates LGBT acceptance and self-love.

Mark B. Stanziola, 56, is a family law attorney with Gardner Law Office in Bethlehem, Pa., where he deals with adoption and LGBT issues and serves on the Board of Directors of the Bradbury-Sullivan LGBT Center in Allentown.

Reflecting on the workplace environment he faced in the 1990s, Stanziola said the stigma surrounding gay lawyers would turn off clientele from seeking their services. Part of the bar exam vouched for a lawyer's moral character and if the person administering the test was homophobic, this could impair a lawyer's reputation or have them disbarred.

In 1992, Stanziola volunteered at Muhlenberg College, where he helped add panels onto the fledgling NAMES Project AIDS Memorial Quilt. When his name appeared in a local newspaper in an article about the quilt, his employer at a small law firm in Allentown approached him about his involvement and asked, "Does this mean you're gay?"

"Then he said to me, and I'll always remember it, 'I'm uncomfortable with your lifestyle change.' Now, I was the same person the day before as I was the day after. The only change was that now he suspected I might be gay," Stanziola said.

Stanziola was confronted with an ultimatum: resign from the job or he would be fired. Ultimately, Stanziola felt there wasn't anything he could do to fight the discrimination case, so he resigned from his job.

He made a point of addressing the audience in saying, "You're probably wondering why I didn't sue for discrimination?" before going on to explain how there were no anti-discrimination statutes in place at the time.

The only anti-discrimination statutes in the 1990s was intended to protect minority groups but did not include homosexual individuals.

"A lot of harassment went on which I'm not so sure this generation recognizes, but even in Allentown, that was somewhat accepting," he said. "There was a lot of discrimination and that lasted — it's still there, but it's less."

He added, "When I lost my job in the early 90s, I was basically a pariah. I didn't quite have an explanation for it. It was a gap in my employment history at that point. It would be hard to explain unless I'm coming out to somebody who could be a potential employer."

After he lost his job, Stanziola started advocating for same-sex LGBT clients and from there, his practice evolved. He started his own small firm conducting legal services for people with low incomes and little access to a lawyer.

"I have that understanding and some compassion for people who don't trust the legal system, who feel that they've been marginalized or that they've been discriminated against," he said.

"Legal services is the perfect place for that … you're dealing with usually disenfranchised people and the gay community usually intersected with it, so it was a good place to be and it gave me confidence back."

As more same-sex marriage bills were passed in the years following, he received more job offers from recruiters. Yet, Stanziola realized these firms could have hired him at any point in his career but were only seeking him for representation following LGBT policy changes.

Despite the U.S. removing the ban on same-sex marriage in June 2015, Stanziola observed that other forms of equality were diminished along the way.

He explained that if a deceased partner left their estate to their partner, they would be treated as a stranger when they claim it and be forced to pay taxes on it. In some states, this would require partners paying an 18% tax on the estate, while a husband and wife would pay zero dollars in taxes.

MARK STANZIOLA

"One day, all of a sudden the Supreme Court says, 'You can get married,' and it was kind of amazing, and then for a while there, all the community was in euphoria that things had changed," he said.

At the prospect of marriage equality, Stanziola said he noticed some people in the LGBT community stopped pushing for other human rights that are still at stake.

Since the Trump Administration came into office, Stanziola said LGBT rights have been pulled back. In some states, people can deny services from LGBT people based on religious grounds, while the rights of transgender individuals remain in jeopardy, including their freedom to fight in the military and access to medical care and public restrooms.

"There's still going to be a big fight, and I don't think we're out of the woods yet, but I think things are better. In my life, I never thought I'd be able to get married. I never thought I'd be able to adopt our son. I never thought I'd be advertised as an openly gay man, lawyer," Stanziola said.

To maintain the progressing momentum for LGBT rights, he said, "If you want to advance, if you want to have rights, you have to be vocal about it. You don't have to be militant, but you have to be at least vocal and visible."

“One day, all of a sudden the Supreme Court says, 'You can get married.' ... ”

WRITING WRONGS 2019 STAFF

WRITERS/EDITORS

Mia Boccher
Rutgers University

Kimberlee Bongard
Ramapo College of NJ

Steven Hernandez
Rutgers University

Kristen Marcinek
Rutgers University

Gillian Russo
Fordham University

Carly O'Neill
Millersville University

WRITING WRONGS 2019 STAFF

ILLUSTRATOR

Veronika Hammond
Montclair State University

PRINT DESIGNER

Claudia Argueta
Kean University

PRINT DESIGNER

Gisell Padilla
Kean University

PRINT DESIGNER

Amanda Maisto
Northampton
Community College

WRITING WRONGS 2019 STAFF

SOCIAL MEDIA MANAGERS

Abby Baker
Rutgers University

Jamilee Hoffman
Kutztown University

PHOTOGRAPHERS/VIDEOGRAPHERS

Sydney Herdle
Penn State University Park

Alexandra Iglesia
Haverford College

Ryley Lehew
Penn State University Park

WRITING WRONGS 2019 ADVISORS

Dawn Heinbach
Founder & Program Manager, Writing Wrongs
Freelance Writer and Editor, New Dawn Enterprises, LLC

Dawn graduated summa cum laude from Kutztown University in 2016 with
a Bachelor of Arts in English/Professional Writing and minor concentrations
in Digital Communication & New Media and Public Relations. She will earn an
M.A. in Publishing at Rosemont College this year and has been accepted to
Cedar Crest College's Pan European M.F.A. in Creative Writing program.

Gayle Hendricks
*Northampton
Community College*
Program Advisor
Print Deisgn

Santo Marabella
Moravian College
Associate Advisor
Writing/Editing

Kathleen Parrish
Lafayette College
Associate Advisor
Writing/Editing

Natalie Shaw
*Lehigh Carbon
Community College*
Associate Advisor
Writing/Editing

Donna Singleton
*Professor Emerita,
Reading Area
Community College*
Program Advisor
Writing/Editing

John Wrigley
Independent Filmmaker
Program Advisor
Photography/
Videography

LGBT+ VOCABULARY

By Sam Killermann, *itspronouncedmetrosexual.com*

Author's Note: "*This list is neither comprehensive nor inviolable, but it's a work in progress toward those goals. With identity terms, trust the person who is using the term and their definition of it above any dictionary. These definitions are the creation of a cultural commons: emails, online discussions, and in-person chats, with the initial curation being mine, then growing into a collaboration between Meg Bolger and me at TheSafeZoneProject.com.*

We are constantly honing and adjusting language to — our humble goal — have the definitions resonate with at least 51 out of 100 people who use the words. Identity terms are tricky, and trying to write a description that works perfectly for everyone using that label simply isn't possible.

Some definitions here may include words you aren't familiar with, or have been taught a flawed or incomplete definition for; I've likely defined those words somewhere else in the list, but I also missed many. This is an ever-evolving project."

advocate

1. *noun:* a person who actively works to end intolerance, educate others, and support social equity for a marginalized group.
2. *verb:* to actively support or plea in favor of a particular cause; the action of working to end intolerance or educate others.

agender

adjective: a person with no (or very little) connection to the traditional system of gender, no personal alignment with the concepts of either man or woman, and/or someone who sees themselves as existing without gender. Sometimes called gender neutrois, gender neutral, or genderless.

ally

/"al-lie"/ – *noun:* a (typically straight and/or cisgender) person who supports and respects members of the LGBTQ community. We consider people to be active allies who take action in support and respect.

androgyny

/"an-jrah-jun-ee"/ (androgynous) – 1. *noun:* a gender expression that has elements of both masculinity and femininity; 2. *adjective:* occasionally used in place of "intersex" to describe a person with both female and male anatomy, generally in the form "androgyne."

aromantic

/"ay-ro-man-tic"/ – *adjective:* experiencing little or no romantic attraction to others and/or has a lack of interest in romantic relationships/behavior. Aromanticism exists on a continuum from people who experience no romantic attraction or have any desire for romantic activities, to those who experience low levels, or romantic attraction only under specific conditions. Many of these different places on the continuum have their own identity labels (see demiromantic). Sometimes abbreviated to "aro" (pronounced like "arrow").

asexual

adjective: experiencing little or no sexual attraction to others and/or a lack of interest in sexual relationships/behavior. Asexuality exists on a continuum from people who experience no sexual attraction or have any desire for sex, to those who experience low levels, or sexual attraction only under specific conditions. Many of these different places on the continuum have their own identity labels (see demisexual). Sometimes abbreviated to "ace."

bicurious

adjective: a curiosity toward experiencing attraction to people of the same gender/sex (similar to questioning).

bigender

adjective: a person who fluctuates between traditionally "woman" and "man" gender-based behavior and identities, identifying with two genders (or sometimes identifying with either man or woman, as well as a third, different gender).

binder/binding

noun: an undergarment used to alter or reduce the appearance of one's breasts (worn similarly to how one wears a sports bra).
binding – *verb:* the (sometimes daily) process of wearing a binder. Binding is often used to change the way others read/perceive one's anatomical sex characteristics, and/or as a form of gender expression.

biological sex

noun: a medical term used to refer to the chromosomal, hormonal and anatomical characteristics that are used to classify an individual as female or male or intersex. Often referred to as simply "sex," "physical sex," "anatomical sex," or specifically as "sex assigned at birth."

biphobia

noun: a range of negative attitudes (e.g., fear, anger, intolerance, invisibility, resentment, erasure, or discomfort) that one may have or express toward bisexual individuals. Biphobia can come from and be seen within the LGBTQ community as well as straight society.
biphobic – *adjective:* a word used to describe actions, behaviors, or individuals who demonstrate elements of this range of negative attitudes toward bisexual people.

bisexual

1. *noun + adjective:* a person who experiences attraction to some men and women. 2. *adjective:* a person who experiences attraction to some people of their gender and another gender. Bisexual attraction does not have to be equally split, or indicate a level of interest that is the same across the genders an individual may be attracted to. Often used interchangeably with "pansexual."

butch

noun + adjective: a person who identifies themselves as masculine, whether it be physically, mentally, or emotionally. 'Butch' is sometimes used as a derogatory term for lesbians, but is also claimed as an affirmative identity label.

cisgender

/"siss-jendur"/ – *adjective:* a gender description for when someone's sex assigned at birth and gender identity correspond in the expected way (e.g., someone who was assigned male at birth, and identifies as a man). A simple way to think about it is if a person is not transgender, they are cisgender. The word cisgender can also be shortened to "cis."

cisnormativity

noun: the assumption, in individuals and in institutions, that everyone is cisgender, and that cisgender identities are superior to trans* identities and people. Leads to invisibility of non-cisgender identities.

cissexism

noun: behavior that grants preferential treatment to cisgender people, reinforces the idea that being cisgender is somehow better or more "right" than being transgender, and/or makes other genders invisible.

closeted

adjective: an individual who is not open to themselves or others about their (queer) sexuality or gender identity. This may be by choice and/or for other reasons such as fear for one's safety, peer or family rejection, or disapproval and/or loss of housing, job, etc. Also known as being "in the closet." When someone chooses to break this silence they "come out" of the closet. *(see coming out)*

coming out

1. *noun:* the process by which one accepts and/or comes to identify one's own sexuality or gender identity (to "come out" to oneself).
2. *verb:* the process by which one shares one's sexuality or gender identity with others.

constellation

noun: a way to describe the arrangement or structure of a polyamorous relationship.

cross-dresser

noun: someone who wears clothes of another gender/sex.

demiromantic

adjective: little or no capacity to experience romantic attraction until a strong sexual connection is formed with someone, often within a sexual relationship.

demisexual

adjective: little or no capacity to experience sexual attraction until a strong romantic connection is formed with someone, often within a romantic relationship.

down low

adjective: typically referring to men who identify as straight but who secretly have sex with men. Down low (or DL) originated in, and is most commonly used by, communities of color.

drag king

noun: someone who performs (hyper-) masculinity theatrically.

drag queen

noun: someone who performs (hyper-) femininity theatrically.

dyke

noun: referring to a masculine presenting lesbian. While often used derogatorily, it is also reclaimed affirmatively by some lesbians and gay women as a positive self identity term.

emotional attraction

noun: a capacity that evokes the want to engage in emotionally intimate behavior (e.g., sharing, confiding, trusting, inter-depending), experienced in varying degrees (from little-to-none to intense). Often conflated with sexual attraction, romantic attraction, and/or spiritual attraction.

fag(got)

noun: derogatory term referring to a gay person, or someone perceived as queer. While often used derogatorily, it is also reclaimed by some gay people (often gay men) as a positive in-group term.

feminine-of-center; masculine-of-center

adjective: a phrase that indicates a range in terms of gender identity and expression for people who present, understand themselves, and/or relate to others in a generally more feminine/masculine way, but don't necessarily identify as women or men. Feminine-of-center individuals may also identify as "femme," "submissive," "transfeminine," etc.; masculine-of-center individuals may also often identify as "butch," "stud," "aggressive," "boi," "transmasculine," etc.

feminine-presenting; masculine-presenting
adjective: a way to describe someone who expresses gender in a more feminine/masculine way. Often confused with feminine-of-center/masculine-of-center, which generally include a focus on identity as well as expression.

femme
noun + adjective: someone who identifies themselves as feminine, whether it be physically, mentally or emotionally. Often used to refer to a feminine-presenting queer woman or people.

fluid(ity)
adjective: generally with another term attached, like gender-fluid or fluid-sexuality, fluid(ity) describes an identity that may change or shift over time between or within the mix of the options available (e.g., man and woman, bi and straight).

FtM/F2M;MtF/M2F
abbreviation: female-to-male transgender or transsexual person; male-to-female transgender or transsexual person.

gay
1. *adjective:* experiencing attraction solely (or primarily) to some members of the same gender. Can be used to refer to men who are attracted to other men and women who are attracted to women.
2. *adjective:* an umbrella term used to refer to the queer community as a whole, or as an individual identity label for anyone who is not straight *(see LGBTQ and queer)*

gender binary
noun: the idea that there are only two genders and that every person is one of those two.

gender expression
noun: the external display of one's gender, through a combination of clothing, grooming, demeanor, social behavior, and other factors, generally made sense of on scales of masculinity and femininity.

gender fluid
adjective: a gender identity best described as a dynamic mix of boy and girl. A person who is gender fluid may always feel like a mix of the two traditional genders, but may feel more man some days, and more woman other days.

gender identity
noun: the internal perception of one's gender, and how they label themselves, based on how much they align or don't align with what they understand their options for gender to be. Often conflated with biological sex, or sex assigned at birth.

gender non-conforming
1. *adjective:* a gender expression descriptor that indicates a non-traditional gender presentation (masculine woman or feminine man).
2. *adjective:* a gender identity label that indicates a person who identifies outside of the gender binary. Often abbreviated as "GNC."

gender normative/gender straight
adjective: someone whose gender presentation, whether by nature or by choice, aligns with society's gender-based expectations.

genderqueer
1. *adjective:* a gender identity label often used by people who do not identify with the binary of man/woman. 2. *adj. :* an umbrella term for many gender non-conforming or non-binary identities (e.g., agender, bigender, genderfluid).

gender variant
adjective: someone who either by nature or by choice does not conform to gender-based expectations of society (e.g. transgender, transsexual, intersex, genderqueer, cross-dresser, etc).

hermaphrodite
noun: an outdated medical term previously used to refer to someone who was born with some combination of typically male and typically female sex characteristics. It's considered stigmatizing and inaccurate. *See intersex.*

heteronormativity
noun: the assumption, in individuals and/or in institutions, that everyone is heterosexual and that heterosexuality is superior to all other sexualities. Leads to invisibility and stigmatizing of other sexualities: when learning a woman is married, asking her what her husband's name is. Heteronormativity also leads us to assume that only masculine men and feminine women are straight.

heterosexism
noun: behavior that grants preferential treatment to heterosexual people, reinforces the idea that heterosexuality is somehow better or more "right" than queerness, and/or makes other sexualities invisible.

heterosexual/straight
adjective: experiencing attraction solely (or primarily) to some members of a different gender.

homophobia
noun: an umbrella term for a range of negative attitudes (e.g., fear, anger, intolerance, resentment, erasure, or discomfort) that one may have toward LGBTQ people. The term can also connote a fear, disgust, or dislike of being perceived as LGBTQ.

homophobic
adjective: a word used to describe actions, behaviors, or individuals who demonstrate elements of this range of negative attitudes toward LGBTQ people.

homosexual
adjective + noun: a person primarily emotionally, physically, and/or sexually attracted to members of the same sex/gender. This [medical] term is considered stigmatizing (particularly as a noun) due to its history as a category of mental illness, and is discouraged for common use (use gay or lesbian instead).

intersex
adjective: term for a combination of chromosomes, gonads, hormones, internal sex organs, and genitals that differs from the two expected patterns of male or female. Formerly known as hermaphrodite (or hermaphroditic), but these terms are now outdated and derogatory.

lesbian
noun + adjective: women who are primarily attracted romantically, erotically, and/or emotionally to other women.

LGBTQ; GSM; DSG; TGNC
abbreviation: shorthand or umbrella terms for all folks who have a non-normative (or queer) gender or sexuality; there are many different initialisms people prefer. LGBTQ is Lesbian Gay Bisexual Transgender and Queer and/or Questioning (sometimes people add a + at the end in an effort to be more inclusive); GSM is Gender and Sexual Minorities; DSG is Diverse Sexualities and Genders; TGNC is Transgender and Gender Non-Conforming (sometimes you'll see "NB" added for non-binary). Other options include the initialism GLBT or LGBT and the acronym QUILTBAG (Queer [or Questioning] Undecided Intersex Lesbian Trans* Bisexual Asexual [or Allied] and Gay [or Genderqueer]).

lipstick lesbian

noun: Usually refers to a lesbian with a feminine gender expression. Can be used in a positive or a derogatory way. Is sometimes also used to refer to a lesbian who is assumed to be (or passes for) straight.

metrosexual

adjective: a man with a strong aesthetic sense who spends more time, energy, or money on his appearance and grooming than is considered gender normative.

MSM / WSW

abbreviation: men who have sex with men or women who have sex with women, to distinguish sexual behaviors from sexual identities: because a man is straight, it doesn't mean he's not having sex with men. Often used in the field of HIV/Aids education, prevention, and treatment.

Mx.

/ "mix" or "schwa" / – noun: an honorific (e.g. Mr., Ms., Mrs., etc.) that is gender neutral. It is often the option of choice for folks who do not identify within the gender binary: Mx. Smith is a great teacher.

outing

verb: involuntary or unwanted disclosure of another person's sexual orientation, gender identity, or intersex status.

pansexual

adjective: a person who experiences sexual, romantic, physical, and/or spiritual attraction for members of all gender identities/expressions. Often shortened to "pan."

passing

1. *adjective + verb:* trans* people being accepted as, or able to "pass for," a member of their self-identified gender identity (regardless of sex assigned at birth) without being identified as trans*. 2. *adjective:* an LGB/queer individual who is believed to be or perceived as straight.

PGPs

abbreviation: preferred gender pronouns. Often used during introductions, becoming more common as a standard practice. Many suggest removing the "preferred," because it indicates flexibility and/or the power for the speaker to decide which pronouns to use for someone else.

polyamory/polyamorous

noun: refers to the practice of, desire for, or orientation toward having ethical, honest, and consensual non-monogamous relationships (i.e. relationships that may include multiple partners).

queer

1. *adjective:* an umbrella term to describe individuals who don't identify as straight and/or cisgender. 2. *noun:* a slur used to refer to someone who isn't straight and/or cisgender. Due to its historical use as a derogatory term, and how it is still used as a slur many communities, it is not embraced or used by all LGBTQ people. The term "queer" can often be use interchangeably with LGBTQ (e.g., "queer people" instead of "LGBTQ people").

questioning

verb + adjective: an individual who or a time when someone is unsure about or exploring their own sexual orientation or gender identity.

QPOC/QTPOC

abbreviation: initialisms that stand for queer people of color and queer and/or trans people of color.

romantic attraction

noun: a capacity that evokes the want to engage in romantic intimate behavior (e.g., dating, relationships, marriage), experienced in varying degrees (from little-to-none, to intense). Often conflated with sexual attraction, emotional attraction, and/or spiritual attraction.

same gender loving (SGL)

adjective: sometimes used by some members of the African-American or Black community to express a non-straight sexual orientation without relying on terms and symbols of European descent.

sex assigned at birth (SAAB)

abbreviation: a phrase used to intentionally recognize a person's assigned sex (not gender identity). Sometimes called "designated sex at birth" (DSAB) or "sex coercively assigned at birth" (SCAB), or specifically used as "assigned male at birth" (AMAB) or "assigned female at birth" (AFAB): Jenny was assigned male at birth, but identifies as a woman.

sexual attraction

noun: a capacity that evokes the want to engage in physically intimate behavior (e.g., kissing, touching, intercourse), experienced in varying degrees (from little-to-none, to intense). Often conflated with romantic attraction, emotional attraction, and/or spiritual attraction.

sexual orientation

noun: the type of sexual, romantic, emotional/spiritual attraction one has the capacity to feel for some others, generally labeled based on the gender relationship between the person and the people they are attracted to. Often confused with sexual preference.

sexual preference

noun: the types of sexual intercourse, stimulation, and gratification one likes to receive and participate in. Generally when this term is used, it is being mistakenly interchanged with "sexual orientation," creating an illusion that one has a choice in who they are attracted to.

sex reassignment surgery (SRS)

noun: used by some medical professionals to refer to a group of surgical options that alter a person's biological sex. "Gender confirmation surgery" is considered by many to be a more affirming term. In most cases, one or multiple surgeries are required to achieve legal recognition of gender variance. Some refer to different surgical procedures as "top" surgery and "bottom" surgery to discuss what type of surgery they are having without having to be more explicit.

skoliosexual

adjective: being primarily sexually, romantically and/or emotionally attracted to some genderqueer, transgender, transsexual, and/or non-binary people.

spiritual attraction

noun: a capacity that evokes the want to engage in intimate behavior based on one's experience with, interpretation of, or belief in the supernatural (e.g., religious teachings, messages from a deity), experienced in varying degrees (from little-to-none, to intense). Often conflated with sexual attraction, romantic attraction, and/or emotional attraction.

stealth

adjective: a trans person who is not "out" as trans, and is perceived/known by others as cisgender.

stud

noun: most commonly used to indicate a Black/African-American and/or Latina, masculine, lesbian/queer woman. Also known as 'butch' or 'aggressive'.

third gender

noun: a person who does not identify with either man or woman, but identifies with another gender. This gender category is used by societies that recognise three or more genders, both contemporary and historic, and is also a conceptual term meaning different things to different people who use it, as a way to move beyond the gender binary.

top surgery

noun: this term refers to surgery for the construction of a male-type chest or breast augmentation for a female-type chest.

trans*

adjective: an umbrella term covering a range of identities that transgress socially-defined gender norms. Trans with an asterisk is often used in written forms (not spoken) to indicate that you are referring to the larger group nature of the term, and specifically including non-binary identities, as well as transgender men (transmen) and transgender women (transwomen).

transgender

1. *adjective:* a gender description for someone who has transitioned (or is transitioning) from living as one gender to another. 2. *adjective:* an umbrella term for anyone whose sex assigned at birth and gender identity do not correspond in the expected way (e.g., someone who was assigned male at birth, but does not identify as a man).

transition/transitioning

noun + verb: referring to the process of a transgender person changing aspects of themselves (e.g., their appearance, name, pronouns, or making physical changes to their body) to be more congruent with the gender they know themself to be (as opposed to the gender they lived as pre-transitioning).

transman; transwoman

noun: a man/woman who was not assigned that gender via sex at birth, and transitioned (socially, medically, and/or legally) from that assignment to their gender identity, signified by the second part of the term (i.e., -man, -woman). Also referred to as men and women (though some/many trans people prefer to keep the prefix "trans-" in their identity label).

transphobia

noun: the fear of, discrimination against, or hatred of trans* people, the trans* community, or gender ambiguity. Transphobia can be seen within the queer community, as well as in general society.

transphobic

adjective: a word used to describe an individual who harbors some elements of this range of negative attitudes, thoughts, intents, towards trans* people.

transsexual

noun + adjective: a person who identifies psychologically as a gender/sex other than the one to which they were assigned at birth. Transsexuals often wish to transform their bodies hormonally and surgically to match their inner sense of gender/sex.

transvestite

noun: a person who dresses as the binary opposite gender expression ("cross-dresses") for any one of many reasons, including relaxation, fun, and sexual gratification (often called a "cross-dresser," and should not be confused with transsexual).

two-spirit

noun: an umbrella term traditionally within Native American communities to recognize individuals who possess qualities or fulfill roles of both feminine and masculine genders.

ze/zir

/ "zee", "zerr" or "zeer"/ – alternate pronouns that are gender neutral and preferred by some trans* people. They replace "he" and "she" and "his" and "hers" respectively. Alternatively, some people who are not comfortable/do not embrace he/she use the plural pronoun "they/their" as a gender neutral singular pronoun.

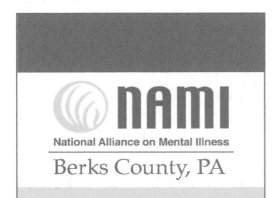

PASSION FOR POWER.

A private, family-owned company operating the largest single-site, lead battery manufacturing facility in the world.

East Penn Manufacturing Company

Innovation

Innovation is everywhere you turn at East Penn. It's in our DNA. It's reflected in our people, our technologies, and our commitment to the environment.

Experienced

Our employees are at the heart of what makes East Penn so amazing. People are the reason we've achieved an annual growth rate that more than doubles the industry average.

Sustainable

At East Penn, sustainability is simply who we are. It's been that way since Breidegam Family opened their one-room battery shop in 1946.

Transportation, Motive Power, Reserve Power, Wire and Cable

www.eastpennmanufacturing.com

contactus@eastpenn-deka.com
+1 (610) 682-6361

East Penn Manufacturing Company, Inc.
Deka Road
Lyon Station, PA 19536-0147 USA

THANK YOU TO THE SPONSORS OF THE WRITING WRONGS 2019 PROGRAM

Sustaining Partner

Townsend Press, Voorhees, NJ

Community Partners

Hampton Inn, Wyomissing

LGBT Center of Greater Reading

Justice Partner

East Penn Manufacturing, Inc.

Honesty Sponsors

NAMI Berks

Patricia Donahue

Dr. Joanne & Kenneth Gabel

Friend Sponsors

Susan Basow

BCTV

Sue Gelsinger

Jodi Greene

Kriti Jain

Kathy Marcinek

Daniel Marcinek

Donna Mitchell

Reading Pride Celebration

Anna Rodkey

Lori Singleton

Nancy Zgoda

CPSIA information can be obtained
at www.ICGtesting.com
Printed in the USA
LVHW062111221119
637822LV00032B/837/P

9 780986 211058